C000092422

IN QUEST OF CATHOLICITY

Malachi Martin

Responds to Wolfgang Smith

IN QUEST OF CATHOLICITY

Malachi Martin
Responds to Wolfgang Smith

Wolfgang Smith

Philos-Sophia Initiative

CONTENTS

To the Blessed Virgin Mary
Our Mother in Christ

Introduction

IT ALL BEGAN the morning of April 28, 1997, with an unexpected telephone call: the host of a radio talk show—the Chuck Harder Program, to be exact—wished to know whether I would join Fr. Malachi Martin in a discussion on topics of mutual interest. Needless to say, I happily agreed; and when the phone rang again an hour later, the three of us were "on the air." The following day I wrote to Fr. Martin, and thus began a two-year correspondence extending into June of 1999, the month before his death.

But why should this exchange be of interest to the general reader? What, specifically, does it contain that is new? A comment by Malachi Martin, dropped in the course of the aforementioned interview, encapsulates the answer. We had been discussing the new horizons opened by science in the course of the twentieth century—vistas undreamed-of right up to their discovery—when the question was raised to what extent Thomism enables us to interpret these new findings, to render them ontologically comprehensible. Fr. Martin replied that to integrate these discoveries into a coherent worldview, Thomistic philosophy alone might not suffice, that in fact "we really need a new Thomas Aquinas." Now these words interested me immensely, all the more since I had recently completed a book in which I prove, with full rigor, that Thomistic principles suffice to dispel the quandaries of quantum physics, the enigma of so-called quantum paradox.[1] At the time, however, I was in the process of completing a paper[2] on another aspect of quantum theory: the phenomenon termed "nonlocality" namely, which had been predicted by a now-famous theorem of quantum physics discovered by John Stewart Bell and was subsequently verified.

[1] *The Quantum Enigma*, first published in 1995 and republished by Angelico Press in 2011.

[2] "Bell's Theorem and the Perennial Ontology" (*Sophia*, 1997), republished in *Ancient Wisdom and Modern Misconceptions* (Angelico Press, 2015).

1

What this result affirms in effect is that *the universe, in its entirety, transcends the bounds of Einsteinian space and time*—a finding Berkeley physicist Henry Stapp refers to as "the most profound discovery of science"! Now, what especially struck me is the fact that this so-called "nonlocality" entails the existence of an ontological stratum well-known to the sapiential traditions of mankind—from the Vedic to the Hermetic and the Platonist— *but virtually unrecognized in the Thomistic.* Not that Thomistic philosophy denies the existence of such an ontological realm, but rather that Scholastic tradition in general has little to say on that subject, and in any case does not give us to understand the enormity of its significance. For this one must have recourse to other traditions, to teachings in fact that have long been impugned by our pundits as "primitive superstitions" and rejected out of hand. And so I came to realize, by way of Bell's theorem, that we do in fact "need a new Thomas Aquinas," as Fr. Malachi Martin maintains.

Oddly enough, the topic of the aforesaid ontological stratum—the so-called "intermediary" domain[3]—came up, as if by chance, in the course of our radio conversation. Knowing that I had critiqued the psychologies of Freud and Jung in my first book,[4] Malachi Martin threw a question my way pertaining to this subject, in response to which I explained that, contrary to the prevailing opinion, Jung proves to be far more lethal to Christianity than Freud: for whereas Freud rejects religion *per se* as an infantile superstition, Jung claims to have discovered its rationale in his doctrine of what he terms the "collective unconscious." What he offers, I maintained, as the enlightened or "sci-

---

[3] The second of what Vedic tradition refers to as the *tribhuvana* or "triple world" which constitutes the macrocosmic counterpart of the *soma-psyche-pneuma* or *corpus-anima-spiritus* ternary. That "intermediary" world, named *bhuvar*, constitutes thus an inherently *psychic* realm. In 19th-century occultism it became known as the *astral* plane, and in Orthodox Christianity it is referred to as the *aerial* world and regarded as the abode of demons.

[4] *Cosmos and Transcendence*, 1984; republished by Angelico Press in 2008.

entific" religion proves in the end to be an *Ersatz*, a pseudo-religion based precisely on a false identification—the most perilous of all!—of the "intermediary" with the spiritual domain. And so, there it was again: *the intermediary domain!* I am constrained to admit that Malachi Martin was delighted with this analysis pertaining to Carl Jung, which in fact encroaches somewhat upon an area of his own expertise. For it happens that Fr. Martin was well aware of the domain in question—to which he was wont to refer as the "middle plateau"—and had personally contacted that eerie realm innumerable times in his capacity as an exorcist insofar as it constitutes in fact the habitat of the demons with whom he was empowered to converse. But let us get back to "the need for a new Thomas Aquinas": we have here a second reason why it is incumbent upon us to broaden our ontological horizon—to open doors and windows, if you will, that have long been shut.

Now, an "opening of doors and windows" is of course what progressivists of every stripe have been advocating for a very long time; the problem, however, is that as a rule they have welcomed contemporary misconceptions in place of perennial truth.[5] What is actually needed is a radically deeper comprehension of the cosmos: the discovery—or rediscovery, to be precise—of ontological strata inaccessible not only to ordinary sense perception, but to the *modus operandi* of contemporary science as well.[6] It will of course come as a surprise to many that there *are* strata of that kind, let alone that there exist corresponding sciences capable of yielding not only insights of interest to philosophers, but applicable knowledge beneficial to mankind. It could even be argued that whereas our present physical and biological sciences cater primarily to material necessities and wants, the aforementioned

---

[5] I have dealt with this subject at length in *Ancient Wisdom and Modern Misconceptions* (Angelico Press, 2015).

[6] The reader will note that I am not counting Jungian psychology as a bona fide science. It was in fact one of my main objectives in *Cosmos and Transcendence* to expose the most harmful pseudo-sciences of our day.

disciplines encompass benefits answering to higher—that is to say, specifically *human*—needs. What stands at issue are the so-called *traditional* sciences,[7] which may also be referred to as *sacred* sciences inasmuch as they pertain potentially to the religious quest. It is crucial to note that in these disciplines it is *man*—the scientist himself—who in a way functions as the "scientific instrument": the microscope or telescope by means of which access to hitherto-uncontacted realms is to be achieved. The enterprise hinges therefore upon the fitness of that instrument, that *corpus-anima-spiritus* compound: its purity, first of all, and its energies—especially those "finer" energies which, in our civilization, are generally squandered in sexual promiscuity. It is not without reason, thus, that the disciples of Pythagoras, for instance, were subject not only to vows of chastity, but to a five-year observance of silence, of non-speaking—something of which we can hardly conceive. But of course, who nowadays understands such things: who is still left in this "brave new world" to whom all this is *not* an "old wife's tale"!

In certain respects the case for traditional science, I am sorry to say, stands even worse among conservative Catholics: the fact that these sciences are "sacred"—that they constitute, in other words, an adjunct of religion—suffices generally to provoke instant denunciation: "pagan superstition" seems to be the canonical term. Now, I have always regarded such a knee-jerk response as unworthy of a Catholic, as un-*katholikos* in fact. But more to the point: I have invested decades in the exploration of such "pagan superstitions," not only by way of written sources, but through personal contacts involving half-a-dozen extended sojourns in parts of India and Nepal, for example, where happily our McDonald's culture had not yet penetrated. And in light of

---

[7] The term is descriptive: these sciences are not "invented" or discovered like our own, but *received* in their essence by way of a transmission, and thus lay claim to a "suprahuman" origin. In the language of antiquity, these sciences derive "from the gods," meaning that they are, ultimately, of *angelic* provenance.

these investigations I am persuaded that there exists a pre-Christian wisdom of supra-human origin, perpetuated in unbroken chains of transmission from master to disciple—beginning conceivably with Adam himself—vestiges of which can still be found in various parts of the world. I have come to believe, moreover, that the wisdom in question—this veritable *sophia perennis*—is something of which we of the present age stand urgently in need. To put it as succinctly as I can: we have need of a *sacred* science because, collectively, we have succumbed to the spell and dominance of a *profane* science that is running out of control. In the face of this onslaught we stand in truth as helpless as a child, without so much as a clue! Even the highest religion, moreover, will not suffice to neutralize this spell or break that stranglehold; the fact is that we are today encompassed and besieged by "*signs and wonders that could deceive even the elect.*" Science, in the final count, responds to science alone: a lower *de jure* to a higher. Hence the imperative need today for a glimpse, at least, of the traditional or sacred sciences, which perceive the universe, not as a mere aggregate of particles hurrying endlessly and to no purpose through the interminable reaches of space, but precisely as the tripartite macrocosm which in truth it is. The case boils down in principle to this simple fact: *Man, the veritable microcosm, has need of his complement.*[8] Or simpler still: "A meaningful life is not finally possible in a meaningless world," as Huston Smith points out.

This brings us back at last to the question with which I began: what is it in my correspondence with Malachi Martin that may be of interest to the general reader? It is first of all to be noted that in this exchange of letters Fr. Martin played a role akin to that of a spiritual director; in particular he did not raise topics of his own choosing, but responded to issues I brought up. It

---

[8] On this question and all that it entails I refer the reader to *Cosmos and Transcendence* (Angelico Press, 2008), and for a glimpse, moreover, into the vistas of traditional science, to the chapter "*Cakra* and Planet" in *Science and Myth* (Angelico Press, 2012).

needs therefore to be explained why I raised these issues: what motivated me in this exchange. The crucial fact is that I felt inclined from the start to submit my—at times seemingly "unorthodox"—conceptions to the scrutiny of this great man and priest, as to someone qualified to judge and to advise. I was eager, at the same time, to continue the conversation begun in the course of our radio interview. From the start I connected the need for "a new Thomas Aquinas" with the desideratum of an enlarged cosmography: the rediscovery of ontological vistas that put to shame the billions of light-years hypothesized by our astrophysicists. And the first step in this enterprise, I believed, must be the rediscovery of the Vedic *bhuvar*, Fr. Martin's "middle plateau." I wanted to share with him my thoughts and intuitions in that regard by way of letters and publications relating to this issue, beginning with the article on Bell's theorem. It was clear to me that, from an ultra-traditional Catholic point of view, much of this material was suspect, to say the least, and that it would in fact be futile to open my thoughts on such matters to "rank and file" theologians on either side of the contemporary divide. I realized at the same time that parts of what I had to say would in fact be warmly welcomed by aficionados of Vatican II[9]; but let me be absolutely clear: I submit without reservation to the authentic teaching of the Catholic Church, which transcends both the pedantic and at times pharisaical narrowness of the extreme theological right no less than the liberal fantasies and pipe dreams of the left. And it seemed to me from the start that in Malachi Martin I may indeed have found the guide and arbiter I had been looking for: someone endowed with both the breadth of knowledge and depth of insight to judge the Catholicity of the views at which I had arrived.

I will of course let Malachi Martin's letters speak for themselves. What I wish to point out, above all, is the human kindness

[9] The major exception being my unequivocal censure of so-called "theistic evolutionism," that darling of the modernists! On this subject I refer the reader to my book *Theistic Evolution: the Teilhardian Heresy* (Angelico Press, 2012).

and astounding humility they convey. One finds oneself in the presence not ostensibly of a savant and polymath, an authority in redoubtable disciplines such as Semitic paleography, but of a humble priest profoundly in love with the Crucified. In dealing with theological issues he seems never to leave out of account the impact the doctrines in question may have upon our spiritual life: whether they conduce to piety and unconditional submission to God, or on the contrary, may prove injurious to our soul. At times one has the impression that he leans to this side or that of a theological issue, not on theoretical grounds, but precisely in the interest of our spiritual well-being. This happens in particular when it comes to the central issue of the celebrated debate between Henri de Lubac and Réginald Garrigou-Lagrange, the question whether there exists in man a "natural disposition for the supernatural": time and again—and notwithstanding his high esteem for Hans Urs von Balthasar, who took the affirmative position—Malachi Martin responds by citing what he terms "the utter gratuitousness" of the supernatural, the fact that "it came as something alien to my nature in the sense that nothing in my nature or the nature of my cosmos made this invasion inevitable or necessary or even possible...." Yet, even so, he did not pass final judgment on this supremely profound issue, but remained open till the end to the possibility that what he had seemingly denied may yet prove to be true; as he writes a month before his death, "I can wait [on this question] in relative tranquility until I am *facies ad faciem.*"

It is to be clearly understood that Fr. Martin's reluctance to concede "a natural disposition for the supernatural"—so far from being indicative of an inability to fathom the likes of Henri de Lubac—stems rather from a deep *pastoral* understanding of what this claim entails. More keenly perhaps than any of his peers, Malachi Martin was cognizant of the spiritual blight that ensues invariably from a careless handling of this issue: from an affirmative response, that is, of insufficient depth. The affirmation of a supernatural ingredient in man is either authentically esoteric or it is rank heresy; and the two are separated by a razor's edge. Think of Meister Eckhart's *Vünkelin* or "little spark" in each and every human being, said to be *increatus et increabile*: "uncreated and uncreatable"! My point is that such conceptions are comprehensible to very few, and that their dissemination to the faithful at large is not only uncalled for but dangerous in the extreme; as Clement of Alexandria has put it: "One does not reach a sword to a child."[10] Now I surmise that Malachi Martin understood this better by far than most theologians, and that this explains his repeated references to the utter helplessness and indeed incapacity of fallen man *per se* in relation to the spiritual realms.

To which I will add—at the risk of trying to say too much—that it is one thing to theologize from the comparative comfort zone of *this* world, and quite another after one has experienced so much as a whiff of the supernatural. Now, in the case of Malachi Martin there can be no doubt in that regard: this priest is no ivory-tower theoretician, no mere *peritus* displaying his theological wares, but a battle-tested soldier of Christ, whose agonies and ecstasies are known to God alone. I have stood in that small room in upper Manhattan—which looks out upon a wall—where for so many years he worked and slept, prayed and said Mass, read avidly and wrote his masterful treatises; and it is all I needed to see.

As to his overall mission, I perceive Malachi Martin as arguably the providential historian of the Catholic Church in our time, whose task it was to bring to light and record for posterity what has actually taken place, much of it "behind closed doors." It was for this that he became at first a Jesuit "insider," the right-hand man of Cardinal Bea no less, and later embraced a mode of life which afforded him the freedom to write without constraint. It is to Malachi Martin that we owe major historical revelations, not the least of which is the disclosure of a Black Mass celebrated inside the Vatican days following the election of Pope Paul VI, an

---

[10] I have dealt with the delicate issue of "esoterism" at length in *Christian Gnosis* (Angelico Press, 2008).

event which seems to have profoundly affected the course of history. Fr. Martin, clearly, was under no illusions regarding the present state of the Catholic Church.[11] He tells us in fact— repeatedly and in unequivocal terms—that in its outward forms and structures it is presently undergoing a near-dissolution: it is "going to entombment," to put it in his own words.

This brings me at last to my final point: apart from whatever human interest Malachi Martin's letters may hold and the light they may cast upon this great man, their paramount significance, it seems to me, resides in the fact that they bear witness to the Church, not only as it was, but also—and especially— *as it shall be*. He seems to have his eye as much on the future as on the past, and gives us to understand that whereas the essential truths of our Catholic faith need of course to be preserved, there are extraneous elements to be shed and artificial boundaries to be razed. Surely all that is orthodox will be found again in the Church that is even now silently forming beneath the rubble of the present disintegration; yet that Church-to-come will doubtless be freed from limitations of outlook and idiosyncrasies endemic to this or that era, as also from the autocracy of any particular theological style: for example, of Thomism as we generally conceive of it. And this explains not only why "we really need a new Thomas Aquinas," but also puts in perspective Malachi Martin's affirmative response to the various "foreign" doctrines with which I confronted him, beginning with the teachings of Jacob Boehme, the seventeenth-century visionary who in the opinion of some has "Christianized" the alchemical wisdom pertaining to the Hermetic tradition. It explains why Malachi Martin could embrace such "suspect" doctrines with unfeigned joy and palpable enthusiasm, and enables us to understand how this faithful servant of the Roman Catholic Church and loyal son of Sanctus Pater

---

[11] On this subject I would highly recommend the eight interviews with Malachi Martin conducted by Bernard Janzen (available in both CD and booklet form from Triumph Communications, P.O. Box 479, Davidson, SK S0G 1A0, Canada), beginning perhaps with *Catholicism Overturned*.

Ignatius could write of that German mystic: "Cobbler and Luthe-ran he may have been by a so-called 'accident' of personal his-tory, but surely Christ bent over him at the midnight of his personal travail…" In place of the customary references, open or veiled, to "pagan superstitions," we encounter in these magnifi-cent words—which in fact echo what Boehme himself reveals regarding "the midnight of his travail"[12]—the perfect receptivity of a mind and heart purified in the Blood of Christ. And who can doubt that this priest speaks, even now, for the Church that is to come!

---

[12] As in midst of a raging storm "I lay on the mountain near midnight"—so Boehme begins his account—"and the Antichrist opened wide his jaws to devour me": at that moment "the holy Virgin Sophia came to comfort me." Here is the passage in full: *"Als ich lag am Berge gegen Mitternacht, und alle Bäume über mich fielen, und alle Sturm-Winde über mich gingen, und der Anti-christ seinen Rachen gegen mir aufsperrte mich zu verschlingen, kam Sie (die heilige Jungfrau Sophia) mir zu Trost, und vermählte sich mit mir."* See Franz von Baader, *Ausgewählte Schriften zum androgynen Menschenbild* (Bensheim: Telesma Verlag, 1991), p. 4.

I

Enter Jacob Boehme

April 29, 1997

Dear Father Martin,

I need not tell you that I have greatly enjoyed our telephone conversation yesterday.[1] Let me just say that it was for me a rare pleasure and a great privilege.

We touched briefly on the question of the "middle plateau." Permit me to share with you some thoughts on that subject which have occupied me for some time. I have tried, without much success, to obtain relevant information from "standard" Christian sources. The most explicit references, it appears, are to be found in the Orthodox literature, which, as you know, refers to this domain as the "aerial" realm. The term itself, of course, is very suggestive; but unfortunately the authors in question treat of the subject mainly from a "pastoral" point of view which does not address the ontological issues that especially interest me. They perceive the aerial world as an intermediary realm to be crossed after death. It is here, as you know, that the so-called "toll-houses" are situated, which appear to be the Orthodox equivalent, more or less, of Purgatory in the Catholic sense. Well, this is all of the utmost importance from a religious standpoint, but fails to provide the kind of "ontological" explication I seek as a scientist or philosopher.

I did however, quite unexpectedly, come upon what I deem to be a major clue. For some time I have interested myself in the doctrine of Jacob Boehme. I don't know whether you will agree with me, but I surmise that it is here, precisely, that Christianity has given birth to a bona fide cosmology. Even as St. Thomas Aquinas has "Christianized" the metaphysics of Aristotle, so has Boehme, it seems to me, Christianized the "Hermetic" wisdom

---

[1] The reference is to a telephone conversation following the radio interview, as mentioned in the Introduction.

of mankind.[2] I would add that Boehme was definitely not a Protestant; his doctrine is diametrically opposed to the ideas of
Luther. But let me get to the immediate point, the "major clue":
Boehme maintains that the creation described in the first chapters of Genesis is not the original *ex nihilo* creation, but constitutes rather a restoration, one could say, of the world or kingdom
of Lucifer, which had been in a sense destroyed—but not altogether annihilated—by his Fall. Boehme makes it a point to
maintain that the remains of Lucifer's kingdom and *our* world
are situated "in the same place"—which seems to imply that the
latter is somehow "superimposed" upon the first. It suggests, in
other words, that the ruins of Lucifer's realm exist to this day
"underneath" the corporeal domain in which we find ourselves,
like some primordial paleontological stratum deeply submerged
beneath the earth. Now, this would explain many things, beginning with the notion—so much emphasized in Orthodox Christian sources—that the aerial realm or "middle plateau" is indeed
the habitat of demons. And it would moreover lend credence, I
believe, to the ontological interpretation of Bell's theorem[3] I have
proposed in a lecture (the published version of which I enclose)
to the effect that the corporeal domain differs from the intermediary by the imposition of *quantitative* constraints, in accordance
with the Biblical verse: "*He set His compass upon the face of the
deep.*" It is, perhaps, as if God wanted to stabilize a world that had
grown dangerously amorphous by virtue of having become dis-

---

[2] In keeping with the "mercurial" nature of its mythical ancestry, it is quite
impossible to give a succinct and univocal characterization of what has been
termed the *Hermetic* tradition (or philosophy or science), which in its historical manifestations encompasses a bewildering jumble of writings ranging literally from the authentically sublime to the wildly absurd. Leaving aside this
welter of ideas, what I broach here as a subject for discussion is precisely the
"Christianized" version or doctrine expounded by Jacob Boehme, which Malachi Martin, as we shall see, characterizes in his response as "a pre-Christian
Christological knowledge."
[3] See "Bell's Theorem and the Perennial Ontology" in *Ancient Wisdom and
Modern Misconceptions.*

connected from its spiritual source or prototype. From this point of view, the danger and indeed the trial of the intermediary domain lies in the fact that there one has been set free from the providential constraints of this, our corporeal world, but not yet entered upon the spiritual: not yet been subjected to the "law of God," which is really to enter into the "glorious liberty" of the beatified.

I have said enough, perhaps, to indicate to you the general direction of my thought. Let me just add that the lecture on "Bell's theorem" was given soon after I had begun to think seriously of "the quantum enigma," and needs to be slightly revised in light of subsequent recognitions. The final paper will soon appear. I am also enclosing my review of an interesting book by a nuclear physicist concerning the cosmology of Jacob Boehme.[4] Yes, I do agree that we need "a new St. Thomas Aquinas" as you have so well said.

One thing more. It means much to me to know that in your charity you will remember me in your prayers. I too, Father, will gladly remember you in mine.

With warm regards and best wishes,

Wolfgang

---

[4] Basarab Nicolescu, *Meaning and Evolution: The Cosmology of Jacob Boehme* (New York: Parabola Books, 1991). Reviewed in *Sophia*, Vol. 3, No. 1 (1997), pp. 172–180.

June 3, 1997

Dear Father Malachi,

As you no doubt know, I have very much enjoyed our telephone conversation yesterday, and am eagerly looking forward to our meeting, *Deo volente*, in August. And so too, let me add, is my wife Thea.

In the course of our exchange you asked a profound question, to which, as it turns out, I gave an insufficient and indeed misleading reply: what do I mean by the words *spirit* and *spiritual*? I responded that these terms bear reference to the "self-manifestation" of God, that is to say, to the Holy Trinity. What I neglected to note is that the term, so far from being univocal, bears reference also to the *cosmic* manifestation. Thus, in speaking of "the spiritual world" (as opposed to the corporeal or the intermediary), one is referring, not directly to God, but to the central cosmic reflection of the Logos, which can be identified, I believe, with the angelic domain. According to René Guénon[5] (who, I must admit, has influenced me considerably), this realm may be characterized as universal or "formless" manifestation, in contrast to individual or "formal," which in turn splits into two distinct degrees: the "subtle" and the "gross," corresponding to what I have termed the intermediary and the corporeal domains. We are left thus with three cosmic levels: gross, subtle, and "formless" or angelic. Now, these are precisely the "three worlds" of the Vedic tradition, named *bhu, bhuvar* and *svar* (once again, in ascending order). It is of interest to note, moreover, that these "worlds" correspond apparently to *Asiah, Ietsirah* and *Beriah* of the Kabbalah, whereas the distinction between "formless" and

---

[5] A French metaphysician profoundly familiar with the sapiential traditions of the world, whose writings have to some extent revitalized metaphysical thought in the West after centuries of decline. Among his numerous books, it is *The Reign of Quantity and the Signs of the Times* that most clearly bears witness to the sheer genius of this in many ways enigmatic author.

"formal" manifestation corresponds, according to Guénon, to the separation of the "upper waters" from the "lower" referred to in Genesis.

As you can well understand, I would love to discuss all this with you at leisure. I come to you as someone eager to improve his own very meager and provisional understanding (if that term is even admissible).

With warm regards and best wishes,
yours faithfully in Christ,

Wolfgang

July 16, 1997

Dear Father Malachi,

First of all let me say that we shall be in New York, God willing, in November, and look forward with what the Germans call "Vorfreude" to the great privilege of meeting you![6]
I have just finished an exceptionally interesting book entitled *Der Begriff der Zeit bei Franz von Baader*,[7] which throws light on the question of "origins" we have touched upon. The author, Ferdinand Schumacher, is a priest, and the treatise was accepted as a doctoral dissertation at Münster, which I take to be a hopeful sign. What particularly fascinated me—among other things—is von Baader's allusion to "eine geistige Christwerdung Jesu"[8] which supposedly took place at the moment of Adam's Fall as an act of divine mercy, and gave rise to a primordial tradition von Baader calls "das Urchristentum." All the most venerable traditions of mankind, he maintains, have sprung from that "Urlehre," which moreover has been transmitted, above all, in the Kabbalistic teaching, and to a lesser degree in the Hermetic.
The Mosaic books, according to von Baader, presuppose this primordial teaching, and are not comprehensible in their full depth without the data it provides. Now, this would mean that Jacob Boehme did not, in essence, introduce a doctrine of his own, but that he rediscovered and restored a lost tradition: reopened doors that had long been shut. I must admit that von

---

[6] It was to be my first—and sad to say, also my last—face-to-face meeting with Malachi Martin.
[7] Franz von Baader (1765–1841), a Catholic savant, was profoundly influenced by Jacob Boehme, and ranks perhaps as the last authoritative representative of a movement, initiated by Pico de la Mirandola (1463–1492), known as Christian Kabbalah. On this subject I refer to "The Wisdom of Christian Kabbalah" in *Christian Gnosis*.
[8] This virtually untranslatable expression refers to a spiritual manifestation of Christ that is tantamount to Malachi Martin's "pre-Christian Christological knowledge."

Baader's thought—which Ferdinand Schumacher has very perceptively disengaged from a mass of almost unreadable text—appeals to me strongly. But let me reserve final judgment till I have had a chance to hear your views.

Yours faithfully in Christ,

Wolfgang

October 23, 1997

My dear Wolfgang,

This is a letter I planned to write to you several months ago. But something happened to me that never happened before. I cannot put it into one word or sentence. But I can express it within the liberty of an unpremeditated letter inspired by what did occur. I have no sense that I am exaggerating when I state that your letters and your book *The Quantum Enigma* together with the sources you opened up to me (Boehme, Guénon, *et al*) constituted a providential source of understanding—the understanding that precisely I had been prepared for (sorry about that proposition ending the sentence!). I must not forget to mention the key role played in this (for me momentous) step by that lecture of yours on "Bell's Theorem and the Perennial Ontology."

Here is the simplest way in which I can tell you what has happened.

Under the stimulus of your April 29 letter, I obtained Nicolescu's *Science, Meaning and Evolution*. Since then I have been plunged into understanding Boehme's doctrine. Yes, he did Christianize the ancient Hermetic wisdom, the pre-Christian Christological knowledge. And his doctrine about the genuine status of our present cosmos is the best formulation of a view I have had since I was put through Hebraic studies at the university. Only thus did and does the Genesis story make sense. Incidentally, has anyone—except Isaiah in his mocking dirge for the Son of the Dawn—ever expressed the terrible ontological shipwreck that Lucifer achieved? I have copied out Boehme's paragraphs for quotation to penitents and to people undergoing both demonic obsession and demonic possession. Boehme expresses such disgust and contempt together with such bitter regret over the spoiling of Lucifer's original archangelic beauty and excellence. Boehme, by the way, strikes a very authentic note in not calling Lucifer an archangel but a member of the Second Choir of Angels (the Cherubim). The Cherubim are the Keepers of God's

20

awesomeness. To humanize what happened, one would say: that almost dreadful awesomeness of God went to Lucifer's head. Hence his revolt.

But, to get back; the next big revelation for me was *The Quantum Enigma*. Please understand where I am, Wolfgang. I know that everything you state is backed up by mathematical formulae. I do not know, I will never know or understand. I claim no progress along that line. What I have derived from *The Quantum Enigma* as well as from your lecture on Bell's Theorem is a very valuable ability to conceptualize what, before this, I intuited and imagined. To use a neologism, you enabled me to ontologize the Creation Narrative in Genesis; I have an intelligible way now of talking about this most fundamental phase of divine Revelation; and that is thanks to you. Of course, I do not understand much—for instance, I have no clarity about that important factor: state vector collapse. Some actual words (*Salniter* in Boehme is an example) escape me. But in spite of my mathematical limits, I have been and am being enriched every day, because now I am plunged—as I said—into these studies.

You have my particular thanks for responding to my question about *spirit* and *spiritual*. The parallels with the Kabbalah and the triple world of the Vedic tradition fit into this picture. I am still inclined to ascribe all such "traces" to the original Hermetic knowledge (Revelation?) which I have always thought of as the pre-Christ Christology. If I do not presuppose this, I find it difficult to account for such wisdom in so many diverse places and sources. Perhaps I am expressing clumsily what von Baader calls "eine geistige Christwerdung Jesu." Perhaps I must wait for the Beatific Vision in eternity before knowing the answer. But surely the Holy Ghost in putting the Words of Wisdom on the lips of the Virgin in her Mass texts does imply an ancient presence before the corporeal presence. Tied up with that mystery is the mystery of the Incarnation: the generation of Jesus as Logos is surely in ontological but not temporal simultaneity with His generation as Mary's son. I must lay my hands on Schumacher's book, some day.

Finally, I want to touch on the central point of my interest,

Wolfgang, in all this intricate material. I asked in particular about *spirit* and *spiritual*; and I asked this in relationship to our discussion about the three levels and, especially, the middle plateau, as I called it. My interest stems from this: *in fine finali*, after all my studies and all my association with the Papacy, with the Jesuits, with the clergy, with the people who have thronged through my life—I am thinking as much of the thousands of newborn babies and of expiring men and women who have hallmarked my days and nights; after all of that, what now fascinates me is the presence or absence of *supernatural* grace (sanctifying grace). And this, for a very selfish reason: my *only* chance of escaping the limits of my mortalness is that grace. What keeps me on the *qui vive*, in this regard, is that this precious thing is totally gratuitous. *Aliis verbis*, the supernatural did invade my cosmos through the Incarnation; it came as totally gratuitous, in no way obliged to enter my cosmos; it came as something alien to my nature in the sense that nothing in my nature or the nature of my cosmos made this invasion inevitable or necessary or even possible—much less probable. Even though it is so gratuitous and alien, I need it—if what I *desire* is to be mine.

You can now gauge how far I am from any really integrated viewpoint. Under the stimulus of your thought and the sources you have opened to me, I now have a solid hope of being able to account rationally for my understanding of the data of faith. When I say *rationally*, I mean *plusminusive* what Anselm said about *fides quaerens intellectum*. And this puts me in your debt; let me explain.

When we as young Jesuits gave *three* years solely to rational philosophy, I had an experience I shall never forget. The physics lecturer (a dull but good and lazy man) flung books about physics at me, and forced me to study—of all things—crystals. I forget the why and wherefore and even the what. The point was that for a brief nine months I had a vision of reality not afforded me by the instructions in what they called rational philosophy—predominantly Thomism. I caught a mere glimpse of the world you have opened. I was in my twenties.

The point I am making really, Wolfgang, is that all I have learnt and approbated since April comes just when I need it; need, here, is of the spirit. And when I say "spirit," I am talking about that mysterious entity, this blessed being—triune of course—that loved me so much.

At the same time, I know that in this letter I have used language both exoteric and esoteric. Even before I entered all this, this year, I was *thinking* outside such bounds, especially when trying (Anselmwise) to understand for instance why Lord Jesus could realistically say, at the Last Supper before He died and rose and ascended, "This is My Body…" Or understand His words to Mary Magdalene in the Garden on Easter morn. Or how I can possibly be associated with Him in enacting Calvary at my daily Mass.

There are a thousand and one scintillations of truth opened up to me like precious diamonds in your scripts and your book as well as in your Jacob Boehme that you have become my benefactor under Christ's providence. All sorts of precious revelations.

I look forward to hearing about your November visit.[9] In the meantime believe me to be your brother in Christ Jesus and among your enthusiastic students and well-wishers.

Always with blessings,

Malachi

---

[9] This refers to our planned meeting with Fr. Martin in New York.

II

Light on von Balthasar

November 26, 1997

Dear Father Malachi,

I will never forget our meetings last week! I find myself at a loss to tell you just how memorable these have been for me. I recall, with the greatest pleasure, our talks, your gracious hospitality—when you treated us to a sumptuous and superb dinner at the Carlisle—and, above all, the joy of being in your presence. I will add that your words of spiritual counsel are very much with me, and will ever be so. I shall do my best, *Deo volente*, to put them into practice. As I have confided to Thea, I perceive my meeting with you as a turning point in my life; and please God, it will be.

Yesterday, on the plane, I read—carefully, and with great interest—your essay concerning Tati.[1] I need hardly tell you that I was deeply moved. This simple tale of a dog and her master, so beautiful and so profound, has brought home to me how little we know concerning the higher function of animals—I am tempted to say, their "spiritual" side—and of their connection, above all, with the angelic realm. What you relate seems also to respond to a perennial need manifesting even in our present disenchanted age: the "braver" our new world becomes, the more ardently many of us will be drawn to the likes of your noble companion—which may in fact be what motivated you to write this essay, this little book. Thank you so much for sharing it with us (I mean here to include Thea and Peter[2]).

Thank you also most cordially for your letter. "Do not be afraid, and do not yield to any spiritual confusion!": I shall treasure these words, which I find to be exceedingly apt. I am also

---

[1] Tati was a dog, a Cairn Terrier, for whom Fr. Martin had a deep affection: "Nobody ever gave me the love little Tati gave me," he confided to a friend. The essay was written soon after Tati's death.

[2] A friend from Switzerland who joined us in New York.

happy to have the two prayers you enclosed, and intend to make good use of them. The literature concerning the SSPX I will share with others.

I conveyed your kind greetings to Peter on Sunday afternoon, just before his departure. Thea and I are delighted to know that you share our high regard for this "beautiful and godly man." As I may have told you, I consider his friendship to be one of God's most precious gifts to me. And let me add that Peter is exceedingly glad to have met you, and looks forward to an opportunity to see you again, be it in New York or somewhere in Europe. I am sure that he would be more than happy to meet you in Rome, for example, if that should be convenient for you.[3]

I am enclosing a number of items, beginning with a letter to Professor Deghaye,[4] along with his response (which I hope will prove legible). The remaining enclosures are as follows.

First, an article entitled "Sophia Perennis and Modern Science," to appear in the *Library of Living Philosophers* volume honoring Seyyed Hossein Nasr, an Islamic scholar who has shown a highly sympathetic interest in my work. Many of the ideas presented in this paper will be familiar to anyone who has read *The Quantum Enigma*; yet perhaps the essay—which was written, not for scientists or the general public, but for scholars versed in the sapiential traditions—probes certain questions more deeply. Getting back to Seyyed Hossein Nasr: thanks to his sponsorship my work has been translated into some of the mid-Eastern languages, and strange to say, is better known in places like Teheran than it is in Europe or America. I was particularly

---

[3] For more on this extraordinary person, see "Remembering a Man of God," *Homiletic & Pastoral Review*, November 2009.

[4] Pierre Deghaye's *La Naissance de Dieu* (Paris: Albin Michel, 1985) has been an invaluable resource in the study of Jacob Boehme's doctrine. See also his excellent article "Jacob Boehme and his Followers" in *Modern Esoteric Spirituality*, edited by Antoine Faivre and Jacob Needleman (New York: Crossroad, 1995).

impressed to learn that scientists in the Islamic world—physicists no less—tend to be far more open to a metaphysical reading of the cosmos than their confrères in the West: perhaps, having witnessed the spiritual blight and cultural devastation that has befallen *our* civilization, they are forewarned, and anxious to prevent a similar catastrophe from overtaking their own. Wherever one may stand in regard to Islamic religion, the fact remains that in regions under its sway, God has *not* been dismissed as optional, nor ousted "from the public square."

Getting back to the enclosures: I have over the years contributed articles to the *Homiletic & Pastoral Review* (courtesy of Fr. Kenneth Baker, the editor), in which I have tried to expose the reader to a metaphysical point of view rarely encountered these days. Now, there is one, in particular, entitled "Biblical Inerrancy and Eschatological Imminence," which may be of interest to you inasmuch as it brings the metaphysical doctrine of "time and eternity" to bear upon certain problems of Biblical exegesis, including an issue exploited by the likes of Hans Küng for their subversive ends. I enclose a copy. And for good measure I am enclosing another—entitled "The Near-Death Experience: What Does It Mean?"—in which it is the distinction between "the three worlds" that sheds light on the subject, leading in particular to an exegesis of Matthew 24:40–41 which may be of some interest.

The most important item, however, which I plan to send you in a few days is a copy of that marvelous book by Julius Hamberger (a disciple of Franz von Baader), about which I spoke to you: *Die Lehre des deutschen Philosophen Jacob Boehme* (München, 1844). The book fell into my hands about two years ago when someone I hardly knew alerted me to the fact that a California dealer in rare books had it listed in his catalog.

I must admit that I feel somewhat guilty sending these many items to you lest they prove an imposition on your time: your most precious time! I therefore feel compelled to add: Please do not feel in the least obliged to examine any of these writings: especially my own (which have already, perhaps, served their purpose in God's providence).

Let this be all for today. Thea joins me in sending you our love and most cordial greetings.

Yours faithfully in Christ,

Wolfgang

January 2, 1998

Dear Father Malachi,

In my letter[5] of December 30th I spoke briefly about "my own greatest problem with Boehme," which concerns his seemingly heretical conception of the Holy Trinity. Ill-equipped as I am for theological speculations of this order, I felt nonetheless obliged to "situate" Boehme in relation to Catholic doctrine as best I can; and it hardly needs saying that I offer these reflections literally "for whatever they may be worth." Permit me to say a few more words on the matter.

Boehme insists that the Son alone is a Person: can we, as Catholics, come to terms with this position, which on the face of it appears heretical? One knows that the Son alone "became man," and may surmise that the Son alone *could* "become man." Perhaps, in light of theosophical doctrine,[6] one can go so far as to say that the Son could "become man" because in fact He *is* Man: "man," to be sure, in a universal and archetypal sense. The same, however, does not hold true of the Father or of the Holy Ghost. But then, if the Son alone is Man, can it not also be said that the Son alone is a Person? The idea of personhood, after all, is normally tied to that of man: in the primary sense, at least, man alone is a person. Not only, then, does it appear from this point of view that the Son alone is a Person, but it can be said by the same token that our "personal" contact with God is in and through Christ alone: *No one comes to the Father except through the Son.*

What about St. Catherine of Siena, someone might object: did she not "converse" with the Father Himself? I think one is

---

[5] It appears that this letter has been lost.

[6] As Pierre Deghaye explains, Boehme's doctrine is not, strictly speaking, a theology, but a *theosophy*, as is also the Kabbalah. See *La Naissance de Dieu*, pp. 18–20; and especially "Jakob Boehme and his Followers," in idem., pp. 211–214.

constrained to admit that such "personal contact" as the Saint may have had with the Father must have been mediated by Christ. This mediation is necessary, it appears, precisely because the Father is not a Person *in relation to us*.

Given that theosophy has to do, as you say, with "the mystical knowledge of the divine," it would thus appear that Boehme's claim is "theosophically" correct: the Father and the Holy Ghost may indeed be "hypostases" in some abstract theological sense—in relation to each other and to the Son—but Christ alone is a person as we humans understand the term: someone, namely, with whom we can directly commune. And so too it is only through Christ's mandate—and thus, through Him!—that we are able to pray to God as "*Our Father, who art in heaven.*" If we were to speak these words "on our own," they would be no more than words, mere "Schall und Rauch": it is through the very Heart of Christ that our prayer ascends to the Father! Moreover, it is only through the mediation of Christ that the Father is "friendly" to us, if I may put it thus: for those, on the other hand, who are not "in Christ," it is indeed a "*dreadful thing to fall into the hands of the living God*"! In fact, it is Hell.

These are a few of the thoughts I wanted to add to my letter. Let me just say, however, that the reservations I expressed regarding dogmatic theology need likewise to be clarified if one is to avoid the impression of a facile anti-rationalism—which of course is about the last thing I would want to convey.

You were very much in our thoughts at Christmas and the commencement of the New Year. As for Thea and myself, we spent the first day of 1998 quietly, enjoying, at one point, a broadcast from the Musikverein in Vienna featuring the annual gala Strauss concert, which this year was superb. How beautiful this music is when it is well performed, and how it captures—as if by magic—the spirit and the very "taste" of the Vienna that once was! One cannot but feel a bit nostalgic. I comfort myself with the thought that all this beauty and "joy of life" will be found again—a thousandfold!—in the world to come.

Again, dear Father, we send you every good wish.
Yours faithfully,

Wolfgang

February 11, 1998

Dear Father Malachi,

I am happy to report that the lecture at Gonzaga University[7] came off very well. Of course, how could it not, given your blessings and spiritual help! I cannot tell you how profoundly grateful I am.

The anticipated opposition—for which I had prepared—did not materialize. This annual Templeton Lecture (which last year was given by Stanley Jaki) was very well attended by both students and faculty, including the Dean, a refined Jesuit who still wears clerical garb. I was impressed by his bearing and manners. In the course of my lecture I sensed that the audience was attentive to every word; there seemed to be a certain "magic" in the air, an angelic presence I like to think. I felt that something was being transmitted and received. The questions which followed were for the most part intelligent and searching, never antagonistic. At one point someone brought Teilhard de Chardin into the discussion, which gave me the opportunity to characterize his doctrine as "science-fiction theology": and even this failed to provoke an antagonistic response. The affable smiles and warm handshakes which followed made me feel that the lecture had struck a chord in many hearts. I might mention that the chairman of the philosophy department evinced a lively interest and expressed a desire to "read all your books and articles," following which he wants to get together with me. He appears to be a Thomist, but I cannot tell whether he is a priest. In any case, he seemed to be probing what I had to say more deeply than the rest.

I enclose a copy of the lecture, plus two other pieces. One is a recently published article in which I take issue with Ananda

---

[7] The 1998 *Templeton Lecture on Christianity and the Natural Sciences,* entitled "From Schrödinger's Cat to Thomistic Ontology." First published in *The Thomist* (vol. 63, 1999), it has been republished in *Ancient Wisdom and Modern Misconceptions.*

Coomaraswamy[8]—whom as you know I hold in exceedingly high regard—on the question of evolution, and the other is another of my *Homiletic & Pastoral Review* articles, dealing with the New Age phenomenon.

I am still reading *The Windswept House*—"savoring" would be a better term. I particularly loved that unforgettable portrait of the Gladstone family. Sometimes I look forward all day to the quiet hour when I can lose myself in the pages of your book: that too I have to thank you for!

Thea joins me in sending our love and cordial greetings.

Wolfgang

---

[8] Perhaps the greatest authority on the *sophia perennis* literature of the world.

March 14, 1998

Dear Father Malachi,

We hope and trust this finds you well. For some time I have been meaning to ask a specific question—but did not wish to disturb you. Meanwhile the issue (which concerns Hans Urs von Balthasar) has come to occupy me more and more. I hope you will forgive me, therefore, if I "pester" you with it.

For long I have asked myself whether there might not be something of major importance in *la nouvelle theologie*: if the Greek Fathers could integrate Plato and Neoplatonism into the Christian worldview, and St. Thomas Aquinas could do the same for Aristotle, why should it not be possible, in our day, to correct and somehow "Christianize" Hegel, let us say, or Schelling, or even Nietzsche? Is there not in each of these German "Titans" a certain spark of truth that needs to be brought out, to be "liberated"? Well, from the little that I know, it would seem that if any among the "new theologians" has something of substance to offer along these lines, it may well be von Balthasar.

Now, as you know far better than I, it is impossible to separate the "mission" of von Balthasar from that of Adrienne von Speyr—a figure I find enigmatic in the extreme. My first impulse, when years ago I had learned a few facts about her and looked at her photograph, was to dismiss Adrienne outright as a mere occultist, a Madame Blavatsky, if you will, in Christian garb. But after reading a biography of the Swiss theologian (I mean von Balthasar), I am far from certain that my initial judgment was correct. One thing, at least, is clear: Adrienne is either a bona fide saint with a major mission (linked to that of her confessor), or she is definitely "possessed." And if she is indeed a saint, then I incline to think that von Balthasar's theology is of great significance, and may point the way to the eventual "self-understanding" of the Church. On the other hand, if she is not, then by the same token I would surmise that von Balthasar's influence—which appears to be on the rise—is prone to be sinister and gravely perilous.

Here then is my problem: I lack the discernment of spirits to resolve this delicate issue. Now, I surmise that you could write a whole book on the question—which obviously I cannot request. But would you perhaps be so kind as to let me know, at least briefly, how the matter stands? If you would simply say, for example: "Hands off!"—I would understand.

I should mention a bit of good news: I have been invited to participate in a Thomistic symposium at the University of Notre Dame, to be held July 18 to 26, the topic of the conference being "Philosophy, theology and science" (which seems to cover just about everything!). Thanks in part to my Templeton Lecture at Gonzaga University—which has been received by the editors of *The Thomist* with undisguised enthusiasm—I seem now to have been "discovered" in the Thomistic world. At long last I can, by the grace of God, be "heard" in these circles; and this, it seems to me, is a great opportunity which I should try to use as wisely as I can. Quite frankly, I never thought I would live to see the day.

Getting back to von Balthasar: I find myself attracted and impressed by much of what he writes. Take the following aphoristic passage, for example: "Our thought and love should penetrate the flesh of things like X-rays and bring to light the divine bones in them. This is why every thinker must be religious." How beautifully he has put it! I am also intrigued by what Peter Henrici has said concerning von Balthasar's philosophy: "It is a metaphysics of love, the outlines of which become clear in the counter-light of a theology of love. Love alone is 'credible' because it is the only thing that is truly intelligible, in fact the only thing that is truly 'rational,' *id quo maius cogitari nequit.* For its wonder lies beyond all that can be constructed by thought; and yet it is no less real, in fact it is the ground of all that is real. Here lies, in both open and hidden fashion, the key to von Balthasar's whole work, and thus also to his philosophy. Only when we succeed in seeing being as love—both as the poverty of eros and as the selfless gift of self—only then do the perspectives of this immense thought come together into a simple and impressive *Gestalt.*" I find this magnificent.

We hope your work is progressing well. And again: please do pardon this interruption! At least I do not indulge myself in this manner too often. Thea joins me in sending you our love and cordial greetings. With best wishes for a most blessed Lent,

Very sincerely,

Wolfgang

March 23, 1998

My very dear Wolfgang, *Laudetur Jesus Christus!*

For your letter of March 14 as well as Batinovich's perceptive review of your *The Quantum Enigma*, much deeply felt thanks. Your letters have always given me much cause for reflection and analysis; the March 14 one is no exception. The main topic, of course, is Hans Urs von Balthasar and his spiritual companion, Adrienne von Speyr, two really extraordinary human beings whose significance necessarily has escaped their contemporaries too busy with the ingrate task of surviving. For no longer have we the human option of flourishing. HUvB and AvSp were both hardy survivors of the debacle. But I am running ahead of my context.

Hans Urs von Balthasar was probably the biggest theological thinker emerging from the Society of Jesus in the 20th century. Big in this context means span of perception and understanding. No one else—none of the so-called huskies in our century—has written so knowledgeably about the theandric mystery of Christ, and done it without offending against basic Christological dogma.

He was the first theologian in a long time who was perfectly acquainted with the original Christian anthropology as it flourished in the first six centuries of our era. He studied them all—Greek and Latin Fathers, was an expert on Gregory of Nyssa (he understood Gregory's theory about the secondary character of our human sexuality) and had correctly assessed the role of St. Maximus the Confessor (the last Church Father).

His patristic knowledge gave him a pre-Thomistic and, essentially, a non-Augustinian optic. So he really was intellectually invulnerable when he walked with his contemporaries into the hurricane winds of apostasy which overtook the Roman Catholic institutional organization at mid-century. He was deeply papist and essentially a Jesuit in spirituality. Father Ignatius—or SPN (Sanctus Pater Noster) as HUvB referred to him—captured his soul entirely, as he did mine. I think Christ, whose

39

vicar the Pope is, decided not to expose this man's soul to the Curial corruption of today, so He designated him to be a Cardinal and then called him home to heaven where he had been preceded by his beloved Adrienne von Speyr.

Our apostate churchmen and devastated priesthood and laity are not ready to assimilate an extraordinary human being such as AvSp was. HUvB wrote one book specifically to assert there was no way she could be separated from his apostolate. Together they founded the Community of St. John (the Fourth Evangelist). She had extra-ordinary charisms, enjoyed a close association with Angels, Saints, the Blessed Mother, Lord Jesus, the souls in Purgatory, on an intimate daily basis. A few generations of Christians will have to pass before she can be fully known and honored.

There is just one possible weakness in HUvB's theology. As you know already, the wildly beating heart of our present apostasy concerns the relationship between nature and the supernatural, between man and God. We know from Christian revelation that God as a supernatural being has irrupted (HUvB's word) into human history and human nature, becoming a man, dying, resurrecting, and now living through His Church.

The dominant school of theology in the Roman Catholic Church today holds that the supernatural is received in the human soul connaturally; the human soul is *in potency* to be supernaturalized. For, the clever modernist argument runs: *quidquid recipitur, ad modum recipientis recipitur.* If I can receive supernatural grace, that "can" implies a potency in me for the supernatural. But if I have a natural potency for the supernatural, I have—in my human nature—some supernatural element. QED. That is why a phenomenologic-ontological analysis of the religious sense by John Paul II concludes that every human being, by the very fact of being *conceived*—yes, even as a zygote clinging to the endometrial wall of its mother—is already *united* with Christ, is already living a supernatural life.

Hans Urs von Balthasar avoided sedulously any such reasoning or mode of reasoning leading to that fatal identification of nature and supernature. Because, as he knew from his theology, it is a dogma *stantis vel cadentis Ecclesiae*,[9] that the supernatural is totally alien to nature. Ontologically, there is no connection between nature and the supernatural being of God. So there can be no *potency* in nature for the supernatural. That supernatural grace is conferred on nature is a case of sheerest orthogonality.

This letter has gone on long enough—to pen an ungrammatical sentence. There is just one stupid-sounding question I have to ask you. I meet the phrase "state vector collapse." Could you give me a rather simplified explanation? It would help a lot.

As a summary opinion about HUvB's significance, here is how I think about him. For those capable of reading him (and her, as a sequelum), there is in his work a very creditable effort to stabilize the triple tensions arising from the human condition (spirit-body, man-woman, individual-community). On the phenomenological plane, no solution is available. Nor finally does the Aristotelian *meson* (*hyle-morphe*) liberate one. Only a God who, as HUvB termed Him, is "a house full of open doors" can promise us liberation from extreme spiritualization and extreme sensualization. I think HUvB envisioned drawing up a blueprint for liberation from the *meson*.

I will assist, hopefully, at your achieving a very deserved vogue as guide, philosopher and spiritual advisor for our effete Thomists and irredentist apostates.

Blessings and love for you and Thea,

Malachi

---

[9] "On which the Church stands or falls"

III

Exploring Jean Borella

May 14, 1998

Dear Father Malachi,

I am still thinking, with much joy, of our phone conversation yesterday. I am glad to know that you are acquainted with Jean Borella[1] and have taken an interest in his work. As you can see, I hold him in very high esteem. He is a philosopher after my own heart, and in his own way concerned with exactly the problems that have fascinated me: for instance, the imposture of scientistic beliefs, and the challenge posed by Oriental doctrines. He is one of the very few scholars in the West with an authentic comprehension of such doctrines as Shankarian Vedanta. On many issues I have—almost instinctively—turned to him for inspiration and guidance; for example, after reading Gilson's *Being and Some Philosophers*, I needed one way or another to come to terms with the Gilsonian critique of so-called "essentialist" philosophy, a stand which would undercut the entire Platonist tradition as well as the Vedantic. Thus confronted with a problem I felt ill-equipped to resolve, I sent off a long letter to Borella indicating my tentative positions as well as my doubts, and in so many words asking for his clarification. He responded to this implicit request—which he received while vacationing somewhere near Lourdes, not far from the Benedictine monastery of his monastic son—with an eight-page dissertation filled with insights of the most profound kind, which has been a great source of inspiration to me. Among other things, it has "saved" me from ever becoming a Gilsonian!

At the risk of sending you a document which may not be entirely comprehensible "out of context," I am enclosing a copy of that response. You will, I am sure, discern in it many traits of Jean Borella, beginning with his marvelous humility. Besides my

---

[1] A contemporary French theologian and philosopher, Catholic and traditional to the core, yet versed in and open to the sapiential traditions of the world.

own Foreword to a forthcoming Borella anthology (*The Secret of the Christian Way*, to be published by SUNY Press), I am enclosing the last three chapters of that anthology in the original French (*Le Sense du Surnaturel*), from which I intend to copy out some other material of special interest to you, along with the table of contents for Borella's first book, *La Charité Profanée*, a work which relates to the Vatican II debacle. Also an English translation of *Symbolisme et Réalité*, a tiny work that strikes me as a masterpiece. Although I do not fully understand its argument, I sense its perfume, its "metaphysical fragrance" if I may put it so.

As perhaps you have surmised, I perceive Jean Borella to be the greatest Catholic philosopher/theologian of our time, a judgment which may be of course highly subjective. What about the mighty von Balthasar, in particular: a man who could, it seems, "size up" Hegel at a glance? What for me tilts the scale above all is Borella's comprehension, in depth, of the Oriental doctrines, beginning with the classical schools of Vedanta. In keeping with my background—my life story if you will—I regard it as the number one theological priority of our times (as I say in the Foreword to *The Secret of the Christian Way*) to bring Catholic teaching into harmony "with all that is true and profound in the doctrines of the East." We absolutely need to recover what Christ termed "*the key of gnosis*" which "*the lawyers*" have "*taken away*": and for this, I surmise, we must turn to the East, where these "keys" have been carefully preserved, not simply in manuscripts and books, but by way of a living transmission stretching back into the mists of prehistory. Now, it is here, it seems to me, that von Balthasar falls short of the mark. From certain passages I gather that his understanding of Eastern doctrines was insufficiently profound: that in fact he lacked the *sine qua non* of *reverence* to access those Himalayan heights, which in truth can only be approached "with folded hands." As to Borella, I surmise he may (like myself) have discovered the East before finding access to the depth of his own Christian heritage: his early association with René Guénon lends credence to this conjecture.

But enough of these musings. I am simply overjoyed to share with you my interest and enthusiasm regarding a philosopher-theologian who has had a great impact upon my thought.

Thea joins me in sending you our love and all good wishes.

Yours faithfully in Christ,

Wolfgang

May 26, 1998

Dear Father Malachi,

I was delighted to hear[2] that you have enjoyed the few samples from Jean Borella's work which I have sent. Today I am enclosing the interview with him, published in *L'Age d'Or*, to which I refer in my Foreword, and which I hope you will likewise enjoy.

I did not wish to impose upon your time yesterday by asking what you thought concerning "*la metaphysique de l'eternelle ostension*": Borella's—to me, stunning—interpretation of the sacred Wounds in the Glorified Body of Christ. From the little I know, it seems that his exegesis goes far beyond what St. Thomas Aquinas, for example, has had to say on that subject. It bears in fact upon what I take to be the deepest question we can ask: the question, namely, *how the finite can be "taken up" by the Infinite without being annihilated thereby.* And let me add that it is on this point, precisely, that I have always felt a lingering dissatisfaction with the Vedantic doctrine. It seemed to me—perhaps due to a lack of understanding on my part—that the Hindu sages are talking "annihilation," an immolation without residue of all that is human, beginning of course with the body, the outermost *kosha* or "sheath." I have queried many a Hindu master on this, for me, burning issue—is it really true that *nothing human remains?*—but never received an answer that satisfied either my intellect or my heart. I have since come to surmise that only a *Trinitarian metaphysics*—and thus Christianity alone!—can answer this ultimate question in a way that does satisfy both head and heart. Now, when it comes to this ultimate mystery of the authentic *deificatio*—I can say unequivocally that Jean Borella has been my intellectual mentor, my guide.

I need hardly tell you that nothing would please me more than to discuss all this with you at some leisure; and certainly I

---

[2] This refers to a phone conversation of the previous day.

Exploring Jean Borella

can come to New York again before too long.[3] But it also goes
without saying that both Thea and I would be delighted if some
day you could grace our house with a visit. Thanks to a kindly
providence we have a peaceful, spacious, and quite lovely home,
set on a hillside at the edge of the Coeur d'Alene National Forest
overlooking Hayden Lake, ringed with forest-covered hills and
tiers of mountains extending northwards into Canada. There is a
spacious guest room and adjoining bath—plus a chapel no
less!—all separated from the rest of the house. If you do visit us,
God willing, we would like to show you the Canadian Rockies,
which are readily accessible by car. And there, from Banff and
Lake Louise to Jasper, one can behold some of the world's most
spectacular alpine panoramas. We took Peter there—a week after
my heart attack, as it turned out—and had a great time.

Of course we will never press you; but please do let us know
if ever you feel that a little outing of that kind might be feasible. I
can assure you, dear Father, that nothing would please us more!

Getting back to Jean Borella: I have written an additional
paragraph for the Foreword to the Borella anthology which "situates" his philosophy in relation to contemporary thought, or
more precisely, in relation to phenomenological thought. On the
chance that you may find it of interest I am sending you a copy.
Let me mention that Henri Bortoft, whom I quote, is a physicist
and student of the well-known David Bohm, who under Bohm's
direction investigated problems of "wholeness" in quantum theory, and later became fascinated with the *scientific* work of
Goethe. He now goes about lecturing on Goethean science,[4]
which in his view belongs, not to the past, but to the future. After
more than a century the world has discovered that when it comes
to science, Goethe was *not* after all a dilettante: my father, who
was a great Goethe enthusiast, would have been delighted! Meanwhile I too have softened my views on Goethe. I am still put off
by his anti-Catholic stance—which at times he expressed in

[3] Unfortunately that visit did not take place.
[4] See *The Wholeness of Nature* (New York: Lindisfarne Press, 1996).

49

terms that strike me as both shallow and impudent—not to speak of his romantic escapades, but at the same time I recognize, more than ever, the sheer greatness of the man.

With our cordial greetings and best wishes,

Wolfgang

June 3, 1998

My dear Wolfgang,
Laudetur Jesus Christus!

Your generosity is even more overwhelming than the richness of
your writings and your thinking—all of which have been filling
my deepest thinking these days. Let me touch lightly on some of
the writings you have sent me, and then dilate a bit further on a
Problematik arising for me from perusing that magnificent
thinker and Catholic, Jean Borella.

His *Symbolism and Reality* is exactly as you describe it: an
extraordinarily penetrating commentary on the modern
dilemma. In it, I think I see the Platonist interpretation in its
most Christian. But, even after two meditative readings, I still
have to go back to it for a fresh read.

Your Foreword to *The Secret of the Christian Way*[5] gave me a
renewed understanding of the very heart of Borella's (shall I say?)
theology. That basic 1950 intuition of his—occasioned, if that is
the word, by the terminology employed by Papa Pacelli in his
dogmatic definition of Her Assumption—is a truly intelligent
way of prying open Borella's thought. Scanning the titles of the
chapters in *The Secret of the Christian Way* only makes me thirsty
to read it all, but especially chapters 8–11. Borella's writing shines
with wayside jewels of intuition as well as proceeding with a rich
river of theological reasoning.

Manifestly, I cannot understand the full implications of his
communication with you apropos of Etienne Gilson. Nor am I
that intimately acquainted with what was peculiar in Gilson's
interpretation of Aquinas. But, I will read the letter again; it is
rewarding.

Borella's *La Charité Profanée* and the *L'Age d'Or* conversation
both illumine his basic theological interpretation, and are precious guides to his mysticism.

---

[5] State University of New York Press, 2001.

51

Likewise the two chapters (11 & 12), which you kindly excerpted for me, expand and dilate on his theology and his mysticism. (I feel uncomfortable using that latter term in his regard, but it is the best I can come up with so far).

Your lecture at Gonzaga University[6] was, in my opinion, a triumph both of clear exposition and a very hardy dissent from accepted viewpoints. That lecture and your essay about Ananda Coomaraswamy[7] have provided me with some solid mental nourishment. Ananda was not accurate.

There remains as the piece which has been with me continuously for four days: Chapters 7–9 of Borella's *Le Sense du Surnaturel*.[8] Here is where my mind is laboring, so much so that I do not think I can clearly formulate what is preoccupying me. But let me try an *esquisse*. What is at stake, in my simplistic language, is the relationship between the natural (or nature) and the supernatural. Borella's thought on this matter, I found, is really set down between pp. 154–157. The traditional theological opinion about that relationship always emphasized the gratuitousness of the supernatural: the natural (or, nature) had no *right* to the supernatural, and no possibility of attaining the supernatural. Supernatural grace is totally gratuitous: I'm not owed it, I can't get it by my own efforts.

Hence arose the classical dilemma: How on earth can I be given supernatural grace? The dilemma is this, in so-called classical Thomistic terms: if I receive supernatural grace, I must have had a *potentia*—otherwise I couldn't have received it. But a *potential* to receive supernatural grace must be itself *supernatural*

---

[6] "From Schrödinger's Cat to Thomistic Ontology," reprinted in *Ancient Wisdom and Modern Misconceptions*.

[7] Despite my high esteem for this great scholar and savant—who has been my mentor in various domains—I wished to point out in the article to which Malachi Martin refers that on the question of evolution, specifically, Ananda Coomaraswamy had been misled.

[8] Geneva: Ad Solem, 1996.

—*quidquid recipitur, ad modum recipientis recipitur*; otherwise I couldn't receive the supernatural grace, could I?

But then that means I, by the very fact of being human (and before supernatural grace is given me), have a supernatural element (not a natural element) as part of my spiritual identity. In other words, there is no such thing as a human being in the state of "pure nature"—*natura qua tolis*. Where does this leave the traditional notion about the total gratuitousness of the supernatural?

It may seem negligible as a difficulty, but look where Borella's notion leads, say in the case of John Paul II, who has always taught since Vatican II that every human being as a simple zygote clinging to the endometrial wall of his mother's womb is already *united with Christ*. The gratuitousness is in jeopardy—the "classical" notion of the supernatural's gratuitousness. In my day at Louvain, we all knew that theologians such as de Lubac, Congar, Chenu, and Malevez privately taught that the human being had a built-in (by the Creator) *potentia* for the supernatural; that, in fact, the state of "pure nature" was a fiction, a nonreality.

For Borella, all is clear. Original Sin is something more than an absence of supernatural grace. His pages 155–156 are capital in this matter. Original Sin consists of the very will to separate nature from grace.

There are gargantuan pastoral conclusions already drawn from this view of Original Sin and man's union with Christ from his conception. The primary one is the absence of any absolute necessity to be a Roman Catholic. I say: *absolute* necessity. Is this why John Paul did *not* [in his *Crossing the Threshold*] say you had to be a Catholic to be saved? Borella drives his point of view to the end, addressing Mary "in whom resides the key to the supernatural mystery of our nature" (p. 157). I could write a book on this glorious subject.

In sum, Wolfgang, I have a lot of spade-work to do before I can integrate the winsome doctrine of Jean Borella into both my intellectual and my devotional-spiritual life.

Give a big hug to Thea, and tell her I am relying on her prayers.

Blessings & affection,

Malachi

IV

From Theory
to Deathbed Confessions

June 17, 1998

Dear Father Malachi,

Thank you for your beautiful letter! Since its arrival about a week ago, I have been much occupied with the points you have made and the concerns you have expressed. I need not tell you how much it means to me to be able to communicate with you on questions so near to my heart.

In your commentary on Jean Borella's work you have lost no time in getting to the heart of the matter, the crucial issue, which you identify as the point of contention in the celebrated debate between Henri de Lubac and Réginald Garrigou-Lagrange. Yes, I see now that Borella's thought in *Le Sense du Surnaturel* does indeed pivot upon the de Lubac thesis, and I recognize too that this thesis leads doubtless to "gargantuan pastoral conclusions" as you say, although I have as yet a very imprecise understanding of what conclusions are actually entailed, and why. Your commentary and articulation of concern alert me to the fact that the problem at issue cuts to the very heart of theology: this is indeed no secondary question! Quite frankly, I was not enough of a theologian—and still am not—to appreciate in depth all that is involved in the issue. Your comments, and especially your reserve, have made me acutely aware of this fact. It is perhaps a great negligence on my part that I nonetheless hold certain opinions relating to the problem. However, I hold these views tentatively, that is to say, subject to correction. I have in the past changed my stand on some very basic issues, and am prepared to do so again.

I am sure it will not surprise you in the least that I concur heartily with your erstwhile professors at Louvain, "theologians such as de Lubac, Congar, Chenu, and Malevez," when they maintain that the human being has a built-in (by the Creator) *potentia* for the supernatural, and that in fact the state of "pure nature" is a fiction, a non-reality. This I can say unequivocally: not for an instant can I believe in a nature "in which there is no

God," to put it in Meister Eckhart's words. Based moreover on my, no doubt very inadequate, understanding of Aquinas, I believe the Angelic Doctor himself would be the first to concur. And finally: is this not indeed the thrust of the "Sinaitic" ontology?[1]

This brings us to the next question: where does this leave the traditional notion regarding the "utter gratuitousness" of the supernatural? So far as grace, or more precisely, sanctifying grace, is concerned, I must be missing something crucial, because, for my part, I can see no problem here. At the risk of making a fool of myself, let me put it this way: Suppose I own a treasure locked in a safe, to which I do not have the key. Though potentially rich, I am actually a pauper—until someone is kind enough to present me with the key. Despite the existence of a supernatural element in the constitution of man, we absolutely need sanctifying grace, and that gift of this grace is perfectly gratuitous. On this last point nothing can ever shake my conviction! Not for an instant can I doubt that without God's grace—a free and unmerited gift, bestowed simply out of Love—we are wretched creatures and hopelessly lost. And yet, for all I know, it may indeed be part of the mysterious plot, the *divina comedia*, that this hapless creature—even here and now!—carries God in itself.

You have touched upon a third question: the "absolute necessity" of baptism. As you know, this has been for me a vexing problem for a long time. I cannot disbelieve the dogma "*extra ecclesiam nulla salus*," because it is *de fide*; yet I am unable to accept it in quite the usual sense, or with the implications that are generally inferred. On this question only one theologian has been able to satisfy both my head and my heart, and that is Jacob Boehme. I have come upon certain texts in the Julius Hamberger anthology *Die Lehre des Jakob Boehme*, which seem to me to supply precisely the missing key to the entire issue. Here is one of these (literally) key texts: "*Vor der Menschwerdung konnte das*

---

[1] The reference here is to the *ego sum qui sum* of Exodus 3:14.

Wort wohl die Seele erlösen, dass sie vor dem Vater in dem Feuer der Schärfe bestand, nicht aber in der lieblichen Wonne vor dem Lichte der heiligen Dreifaltigkeit. Die Wiederkunft aus dem Grabe war hier nicht zu erreichen; sollte der Mensch aus dem Grabe erstehen, so musste das Wort erst Mensch werden."[2] Here Boehme distinguishes evidently between a salvation "of the soul" and the integral salvation promised by Christ: what a profound and wonderful distinction! And what a flood of light this sheds upon the Oriental religions! To my mind, it resolves the seemingly insoluble problem posed by the dogma of exclusive salvation. Yes, outside the Church there is no integral salvation, no salvation of the man, the compound of body and soul. And yet the Hindus, for example, also partake of Christ: "*Nicht im Wesen, sondern (blos) in der Kraft; nicht im Fleische, sondern (blos) im Geiste,*"[3] as Boehme explains.

How sweet these words are to my ears! And how grating, by comparison, the words of Boniface VIII: "to be entirely subject to the Roman Pontiff is necessary for salvation"—so long, of course, as one understands them in their literal sense.

On July 18 I am scheduled to leave for Notre Dame to give a lecture (the same I gave at Gonzaga) the following day. I shall call you before I leave, if I may, to ask your advice.

Today Thea is very happy. She tells me she has discovered an ancient *Salve Regina* (dated 1024) that is simply "out of this world." So beautiful! Thea is never more in her element than when occupied with the great music of the Church. It is very much "in her bones."

---

[2] "Before the Incarnation the Word was able indeed to save the soul, so that it could endure before the Father in the Fire of His severity, but not in the Bliss before the light of the Holy Trinity. The resurrection from the grave could not be achieved; if man was to rise from the grave, the Word needed to become man." (op. cit., p. 185)

[3] "Not in nature, but (merely) in power; not in the flesh, but (merely) in spirit" (op. cit., p. 185).

A couple of days ago I received a letter from Jean Borella which I think may interest you. It is definitely not my usual practice to pass on letters, but in your case I am more than happy to make an exception. A long time ago—before I heard from you on the subject—I had written to Borella asking him what he thought of Hans Urs von Balthasar and Adrienne von Speyr; and here, at last, is his reply. I surmise you will agree heartily with all he has to say. A copy of the letter is enclosed.

Thank you again, dear Father, for this precious opportunity to communicate with you on questions which, as you can see, occupy me deeply. We trust and hope your summer is progressing well. Thea joins me in sending you our best wishes and our warmest regards.

Yours faithfully in Christ,

Wolfgang

June 25, 1998

My very esteemed and wise Wolfgang,
Laudate Jesus Christus!

It seems to the superstitious little Irishman in me that God could only have decided to make me the recipient of so much unexpected enlightenment through your benign generosity because He has for some reason or other predestined me to see His Holy Face in eternity. Else, why squander such pearls?

This is my way of saying, of course, that the input (horrible modern word, but it will do) afforded me by the spate of literature (mainly Borella) I now enjoy, supplemented by your copperplate reasoning in letters, and enriched by those superb letters of Jean Borella, that all this has made a distinct difference in me during my seventy-seventh year of life.

Until I have finished an autobiographical sketch, it will not be possible for me to attempt to tell you what a *profound* difference both your mode of reasoning as well as the content of your thought have made in having brought to a satisfactory close a search I have been on for nearly forty years. I speak of my interior man, my soul as a priest and as a human being. But in good time you will get that autobiographical sketch.[1]

The additional parts of Jean Borella's *Sense du Surnaturel* as well as your commentaries are of tremendous aid and *light*. As a priest and as a working member of a Roman Service I have to make and implement grave decisions affecting the salvation of many souls. Today, the gravest concern the *supernatural* and the preservation of genuine Roman Catholic belief in the face of any genuine ecumenism (and we cannot get away from ecumenism; John Paul II has seen to that), in the face of what the Church (not Church*men* but the Church) can authoritatively demand from believers as conditions *sine qua non* to assure their eternal salvation. Only too vividly, Wolfgang, do I realize from the multiple

---

[1] Sad to say, I never did.

deathbed confessions I have to conduct, how pathetically dependent the dying person is on the very basics, as the already worn strings of life start snapping, and the end comes.

So, of course, I have Anselm's *fides quaerens intellectum*, but I must balance that with the *pauper sum et peccator expectans misericordiam*. And grace, His grace, does the needful.

I want to end here, momentarily. But when I have read some more and thought some more, I shall communicate.

My blessings over Thea and yourself. Someday I would like to hear that *Salve Regina*. By the way, I did not thank you for several pieces—the *Sophia* piece about Ananda Coomaraswamy, and the others; but more about all that later.

Blessings & affection & esteem,

Malachi

V

The Kinship
Between Boehme
and St. John of the Cross

The Kinship Between Boehme and St. John of the Cross

November 18, 1998

Dear Father Malachi,

We hope and trust this finds you well. Just a year has passed since we had the honor and great good fortune to see you in New York—a meeting we love to recall!

Enclosed is an article on *"himmlische Leiblichkeit"*[1] which I have wanted to write for a long time. I hope you will like it. Please correct me if I am wrong, but I have the impression that "celestial corporeality" has not been dealt with adequately in the mainstream Catholic theological literature: as I say in the paper, there is reason to surmise that the subject comes into its own precisely in the doctrine of Jacob Boehme.

Now, I have a problem concerning which I would very much like to ask your advice, if I may. I am tempted to voice my thoughts concerning *himmlische Leiblichkeit* before a conservative Catholic audience, but am not sure at all that this would be a good idea. Bill Carroll, in particular, has invited me to lecture at a symposium he is organizing at Cornell College in Iowa, and the thought has crossed my mind that I might speak on celestial corporeality along the lines of my article. But I have no idea—not a clue!—how he and his predominantly Thomistic colleagues would react. The doctrine of Boehme may come to them as quite a shock: it is no small thing, after all, to be told that "Boehme's God comes to birth in Hell"![2] And besides, why would a Catholic audience be interested in the views of a seventeenth-century

---

[1] "Celestial Corporeality"; reprinted in *Ancient Wisdom and Modern Misconceptions*.

[2] This temerarious quotation from Pierre Deghaye, *La Naissance de Dieu ou la Doctrine de Jacob Boehme*, needs of course to be elucidated. For a brief explanation I refer the reader to *Ancient Wisdom and Modern Misconceptions*, pp. 78–84. See also "The Gnosis of Jacob Boehme," in *Christian Gnosis*, which provides an introduction to Jacob Boehme and an overview of his doctrine.

Lutheran cobbler?! And finally, my base of support in the Catholic world (if indeed I have any) lies in the Thomistic community, which is obviously centered upon the teachings of St. Thomas Aquinas. It was my Gonzaga lecture "From Schrödinger's Cat to Thomistic Ontology," after all, that opened the doors at Notre Dame. To make it clear, so soon, that I am *not* a dyed-in-the-wool Thomist might be unwise. On the other hand, I believe in truth: in the power and majesty of ideas that derive from on high; and I need not tell you that I incline to view Jacob Boehme as indeed a prophet (regardless of whether he is so, technically speaking, or not). It appears to me that he has revealed a truth about God that lies outside the focus of dogmatic theology—and yet affects absolutely everything! If there be such a thing as a "scientific" theology—in the high sense, naturally, of "Wissenschaft" as opposed to our plodding "science" of the Baconian kind—it can be none other, I presume, than Boehme's theosophy.[3]

Now, if such be indeed the case, is it not high time to make Boehme's doctrine known in the Catholic world? Does not the Church—presently reeling under the sway of a profane science which has transgressed its rightful bounds—have need precisely of that truth? If a lower science has caused its downfall—as to a considerable extent it already has—might not a higher be indeed called for? I recall a profound comment you made during our erstwhile radio interview: "We really need a new Thomas Aquinas," you said: how very true! And I am wondering whether *"der Gottselige und hocherleuchtete Jacob Boehme"*[4]—as it says on the title page of my 1715 Boehme edition—might not be our man.

So there you have the counter-argument. The trouble is: if I do present what I have to say on this subject, who will listen to

---

[3] It should however be noted that "theology" and "theosophy" constitute different genres, as Pierre Deghaye points out, in consequence of which the two disciplines are not directly comparable. A great deal of confusion and misunderstanding can be obviated if one bears this basic fact in mind.

[4] "The godly and highly illumined Jacob Boehme"

me? Thea has told me repeatedly: "First make a name for yourself, then speak your mind." Yes, but after all these years I still do not have a "name" that could carry even a fraction of the weight: I feel lucky just to have crossed the portals of the Jacques Maritain Institute at Notre Dame! One false step and out I go.

One more point. Perhaps my Thomistic friends would be only too glad to consider my tenets on the subject of "celestial corporeality"; perhaps they would welcome an influx of new ideas, thrilled to contemplate a notion of "immortality" that seems to connect even with insights stemming from Einstein's theory! Yes, *perhaps*; but as I have said before, I have actually not a clue.

This, then, is my predicament; and I would be most grateful to you for any comment or advice that might help me to break the deadlock.

I trust you have received our greetings from Vienna. It was an interesting visit. We drove out to the residential quarter where I grew up, and stood before the old house at Blaasstrasse 30— which now seemed much smaller to me than it had some sixty years ago. All of Vienna, in fact, seemed somehow "smaller"— except for the glorious St. Stephen's Cathedral! But even here I was disappointed. Not, to be sure, in the cathedral itself, but first of all in the music: how pitiful! What have they done with the musical treasures of our Catholic heritage—and in Vienna, of all places! We attended three Masses in all. At the first the priest was attired in what looked to me like an old lady's dressing gown; I have never seen anything like it! And at another Mass we were told in the course of the sermon that the early Christians—St. Paul included—expected an imminent Parousia, a notion these priests have presumably picked up from Hans Küng. (I should send them my article on "Biblical Inerrancy and Eschatological Imminence.") But then, I hardly need to tell *you* what is happening these days!

On the positive side: we had a memorable dinner at the Drei Hussaren off the Kärntnerstrasse—how we would love to invite you there! Not to mention an evening at the Staatsoper, and even better, a concert at the Musikverein—where absolutely nothing has changed since the days when my parents used to sit in those very velvet-covered seats...

Thea joins me now in sending our warm regards and best wishes for a very happy Thanksgiving! We shall be lifting a glass to you.

Yours cordially,

Wolfgang

November 24, 1998

Dear & Treasured Wolfgang,
Laudetur Jesus Christus!

Your letter of November 18 provided me with two luxuries: an intellectual feast filling up lacunae which traditional Thomism leaves in our assessment of Trinitarian being; and a spiritual (meaning, by that, a supernatural) perception into the sheer beauty of that central focus of our belief (and Christ's full revelation to us), namely our adorable God (Father, Son, Holy Spirit), in all the infinite detail of mysterious being.

On the way, you provided me with a thumbnail outline of Boehme's vision—cobbler and Lutheran he may have been by a so-called "accident" of personal history, but surely Christ bent over him at the midnight of his personal travail and poured in the blessed light of His Holy Spirit all over Boehme's faculties. At least that is how I look on Boehme: a very Holy Spirit-enlightened man destined by Christ the Revelator of God's mystery to indicate to us of the latter days when and how we can fill out our understanding of God.

I take it as not accidental that today (when I finished my third reading of your paper)[5] is the feast of St. John of the Cross. I have been a student of St. John for over 50 years. And on rereading his materials, I realize he would be the first to use the Boehmian conceptuology and terminology, the *Ungrund*,[6] the function of *darkness*, the meaning of *light*, and so forth, in order to convey his mystical doctrine of the Dark Night—his hallmark teaching.

I take it that this paper will be published in *Sophia*. And I pray it shall. I also want to ask you: does that journal supply what we used to call "offprints" of articles, i.e., separate copies of the

---

[5] The reference is to "Celestial Corporeality."
[6] Something intrinsically unknowable that underlies the *Grund*, the Ground of *being*.

article? If not, in any case, I intend to purchase copies of *Sophia*, because I would like to send them abroad to European friends.

Now as to your all-important question, here is my judgment. You will never be taken as a dyed-in-the-wool Thomist. Nor should you be, because your excellence lies in bringing a very acute and informed intellect to bear on the impasse into which Roman Catholic intellectualism has been trapped for these many years. Precisely, the refreshing insights of Boehme could deblock that impasse and let Roman Catholic intellectualism breathe in fresher spaces.

So I think you should accept the Cornell College invitation. Of course, there would be some caveats so that you avoid any misunderstandings; and, if you wished, I could indicate the caveats and precautions I think are indicated.

I should end here so that you can have this letter. My rehabilitation since my stroke in August progresses slowly and steadily. By February-March 1999, I should have a return of control over arm and leg.

Blessings on you and Thea. May the Lord Jesus give you all the light you need.

Love,

Malachi

VI

Concerning the Kabbalah

December 7, 1998

Dear Father Malachi,

Ever since we received your letter last Saturday our thoughts have been with you. I need not tell you that Thea and I were shocked and grieved by the news you mentioned so casually near the end of your letter! But we feel reassured by your report, the good recovery you have made, and are continuing to make. We pray that it will be speedy and complete.

I am wondering whether this traumatic event may not be viewed as a sign from on high that you should henceforth moderate your labors and exertions—which a lesser man could not support for so much as a week even in his prime! If I may say so: I don't think anything less than what did happen could have convinced you of this necessity. In any case, we thank God you have not suffered any serious impairment, and are now well on the road to a complete recovery: *Gott sei Dank*!

How kind of you to respond—in such detail, and with such profound eloquence—to my query! Needless to say, if I had known of your convalescence I would never have troubled you with my request. Yet I am delighted to have your letter, which is a beautiful and inspiring document in its own right. I cannot tell you how much it means to me to have your wholehearted support in regard to the theological position I espouse. I sense that you bring to bear upon the issues at hand a spiritual perception which I, a mere theoretician, am incapable of. And you go on to express that marvelous perception in language I find marvelous as well—as when you speak of Christ bending over our German mystic "at the midnight of his personal travail"! How wonderful it would be, let me add, if someone were to write a treatise on the connection between Jacob Boehme and St. John of the Cross!

I was very happy, too, that you have given me the "green light" to share my thoughts on the matters in question with my Thomistic friends: this is what I was actually hoping to hear. When the time comes, moreover, I shall be most grateful to you

73

for those "caveats and precautions" to which you allude. Meanwhile I am sending a copy of my *Sophia* article to Bill Carroll, with the suggestion that this be my subject at the upcoming conference. The original understanding, I should point out, was that I speak simply on "time and eternity," presumably in a Thomistic strain.

Incidentally, I intend to find out whether *Sophia* offers reprints, in which case I shall order some. If not, I will be glad to order for you however many copies of the journal you would like; I would also be happy to run off some xerox copies.

Your beautiful words, spoken in the course of our phone conversation, are still ringing in my ears. I thank you with all my heart for this warm and exceedingly generous approval and expression of support.

We have had a mild autumn this year. But now at last some snow has fallen, enough to whiten the surrounding hills. I find it a lovely time of the year—although Thea much prefers her San Diego climate, with flowers in bloom all winter long.

Thea is writing to you under separate cover. She joins me today in sending you our love. You are ever in our prayers and in our heart.

With every good wish,

Wolfgang

December 15, 1998

Dear Father Malachi,

First of all let me apologize to you for something I said in my let-ter of December 7: it was not my place to speculate on the signif-icance of recent events in your life, and in retrospect I don't like the sound of the two sentences in question. I ask you now to gra-ciously wipe this incident off the slate—as in the beautiful story from the life of St. Margaret Mary Alacoque which you related when we had lunch at the Plaza.

In recent days I have had occasion to reflect on the connec-tion between Jacob Boehme and the Kabbalah. On perusing some of my books I am struck by the closeness of that connec-tion, which seems to verge upon identity. I love the anecdote related by Friedrich Christian Oetinger in his autobiography. One day, when he was still a young man (it must have been in the 1720's), he approached the eminent Kabbalist Koppel Hecht of Frankfurt to ask how he might attain to an understanding of the Kabbalah, whereupon the latter referred him to someone who wrote on that subject "more openly than the *Zohar*"—and that was none other than our Jacob Boehme.

You may recall that I have had occasion to mention Avice-bron in my paper on "celestial corporeality." I had quite forgotten that I have a book dealing with the philosophical writings of Avi-cebron (under his real name, which is Solomon Ben Yehudah Ibn Gebirol) that brings to light the Kabbalistic basis of his doctrine. It turns out that the philosopher who gave that magnificent defi-nition of "super-materiality" also believed, with Boehme, that "the human body [as it now exists] is a later condensation of the original body, which was composed of Light"!

As you can well understand, I am fascinated by these revela-tions. And I realize that everything I said in the last two sections of my paper could be based on the Kabbalah as well. It occurred to me, therefore, that in my proposed presentation at Cornell College I may simply summarize the basic Kabbalistic conceptions I need for my discussion of *himmlische Leiblichkeit*, and then proceed to develop that notion. It may be that with a Catholic audience the Kabbalah will carry more weight than would the speculations of a non-Catholic mystic: after all, one knows that Albertus Magnus held Avicebron in high esteem, and that St. Thomas quoted Maimonides profusely, and always with respect.

If I were younger, how I would love to follow in your footsteps to learn Hebrew, and delve into the Kabbalistic literature—without of course forgetting Jacob Boehme. Actually, it seems to me that Kabbalah, Hermeticism, and the doctrine of our German mystic can hardly be separated. These three legacies seem to form one underlying tradition, one grand perennial doctrine which, as you say, springs from Christ Himself. What Boehme has done is to expound that doctrine more openly, and in overtly Christian terms. Perhaps, thanks to him, the Catholic Church will one day make the Kabbalah its own. Or better said: will recognize the Kabbalah *to be* its own![1] And I wonder whether perhaps it will be on the basis of this assimilated Kabbalah that the Church will eventually resolve the enigma of the "separated religions," and in so doing will realize her own authentic and ultimate Catholicity.

Permit me to share with you a few quotations which you may enjoy. The first comes from a book by Gershom Scholem.[2] After pointing out that the Hebrew words *'or* (light) and *ras* (mystery) have the same numerical value 207, he goes on to say: "*So spiegelt sich der Glanz des göttlichen Lichtes, das in der Tora scheint, in den Mysterien dieses Buches wieder. Als diese Mysterien jedoch unter der Verkleidung des Wortsinns erscheinen, verdunkelt sich ihr Licht. Der Wortsinn der Tora ist Dunkelheit, aber der kabbalistische Sinn, das Mysterium, ist der 'Sohar', der in jeder Zeile*

---

[1] Actually that recognition occurred long ago when Cardinal Egidio di Viterbo (1465–1532), a so-called Christian Kabbalist, referred to the Kabbalah as "not foreign, but domestic." See "The Wisdom of Christian Kabbalah" in *Christian Gnosis*.
[2] *Zur Kabbala und ihrer Symbolik* (Zürich: Rhein-Verlag, 1960).

der Schrift aufleuchtet."[3] Is this not marvelous? Here too, it seems, one can say: "*The light shineth in darkness…*"

Next, let me give a quotation from the *Zohar* (Book I): "The primal center is the innermost light, of a translucence, subtleness, and purity beyond comprehension. That inner point extended becomes a 'palace' which serves as an enclosure of the center, and is also of a radiance translucent to an incomprehensible degree. The 'palace' vestment for the incognizable inner point, while it is an unknowable radiance in itself, is nevertheless of a lesser subtleness and translucency than the primal point. The 'palace' extends into a vestment for itself, the primal light. From thence outward, there is extension upon extension, each constituting a vestment to the one before, as a membrane to the brain. Though membrane first, each extension becomes brain to the next extension." I am particularly struck by the phrase: "from thence outward." It seems to me to betoken the point of inversion: the point where "intensive" extension[4] becomes extensive, that is to say, *quantitative.*

One more quotation, if I may (this too comes from Book I of the *Zohar*): "Rabbi Isaac said: At the Creation, God irradiated the world from end to end with the light, but then it was withdrawn, so as to deprive the sinners of the world of its enjoyment, and it is stored away for the righteous, as it stands written: '*Light is sown for the righteous*' (Ps. 97:11); then will the worlds be in harmony and all will be united into one; but until the future world is set up, this light is put away and hidden. This light emerged from the darkness which was hewed out by the strokes of the Most Secret; and likewise, from the light which was hidden away,

---

[3] "Thus the luster of the divine light that shines in the Tora is mirrored in the mysteries of this book. But since these mysteries appear under the disguise of the literal sense, their light is darkened. The literal sense of the Tora is darkness, but the kabbalistic sense, the mystery, is the '*Sohar*,' which shines through every line of the text."

[4] The notion of "intensive extension" (which derives from Julius Hamberger, a disciple of von Baader) is developed in my article on "Celestial Corporeality."

through some secret path, there was hewed out the darkness of the lower world in which inheres the light. This lower darkness is called 'night' in the verse, '*and the darkness He called night*' (Gen. 1:5)." Now, is this not in essence the "triple cosmology" of Jacob Boehme?

We hope, please God, that your recovery is continuing to progress well, and pray daily for that intention.

With our love and warm wishes,

Wolfgang

Concerning the Kabbalah

December 1998[5]

Dear Wolfgang,

An immediate reaction to yours of December 15. When you mentioned Ibn Gebirol, I looked him up, and of course saw what you see. Boehme, Kabbalah and the Hermetic strain cannot be separated, as you say. The Rabbis realized that there was a special reason why the FIRST creation of God was Light: "*Let there be light.*" And I know you read that last quotation from Book I of the *Zohar* in relation to the Prologue to the Fourth Gospel.

God, the Light, surely acted through Boehme, Rabbi Isaac and Ibn Gebirol and others. You now have a great opportunity to explain the unity of the mystical knowledge of the divine as distinct from the rational. I do believe John of the Cross with his doctrine of Light and Darkness belongs in this explication.

The Kabbalah connection is obvious. Interestingly, the root-word in Semitic, QBL, has the same basic signification as the Greek καταλαμβανο which John the Evangelist uses in regard to man's incapacity/non-reception/rejection of the LIGHT. The Gematric value of 'OR and RAS was important to the Rabbis. But the best among them used Gematric[6] values, not as *normative* of meaning, but as *confirmative.*

In a previous letter I mentioned certain caveats and precautions in expounding this magnificent theme to a Roman Catholic audience. After the New Year's beginning, let me drop you a few lines about this matter.

Blessings, again, on you and Thea.

Love,
Malachi

---

[5] This letter was written, not on stationary, but on a card, and carries no exact date.
[6] On the Kabbalistic science called *Gematria*, I refer the reader to *Christian Gnosis*, especially pp. 105–112.

VII

The Need
for a "Healthy" Esoterism

December 30, 1998

Dear Father Malachi,

Thank you very much for your kind greetings, as also for your most welcome response regarding Jacob Boehme and the Kabbalah. You were especially in our thoughts and prayers at Midnight Mass.

I am struck and delighted by your allusion to "the unity of the mystical knowledge of the divine as distinct from the rational." This, it seems to me, is truly the point of it all. On the plane of the authentic "mystical knowledge of the divine" there is unity. And this is what theosophy (in the true sense of this much-abused term) is about: it has to do precisely with *mystical knowledge of the divine*. Historically speaking, there are of course different theosophical doctrines, which to the mere scholar may seem to diverge in this or that regard; and yet I surmise that the true mystics understand one another perfectly: on that plane, as you say, there is unity. But that unity does not descend to the rational level: that is where the problem lies. And that must be the reason why theosophy is not compatible with dogmatic theology, as Deghaye points out. It would appear that dogmatic theology, by virtue of its rational approach, entails certain limitations. One could perhaps say that it is unable to transcend the relativity of its own perspective. I am reminded of the final instruction St. Thomas imparted to his friend and faithful disciple Reginald—the "*mihi ut palea videtur*"[1]—which seems to have almost universally fallen upon deaf ears, not the least among Thomists. When the Master laid down his pen forever and confided to Reginald that all he had written is "mere straw"—was he not in fact declaring the inherent limits of dogmatic theology as such compared with "the mystical knowledge of the divine"?

I was interested in the concordance between the Semitic root QBL and the Greek *katalambano*, which you have pointed out. I

[1] "To me appears as straw."

83

find that the Greek word occurs in St. John's Gospel just twice: in John 1:5 and 12:35, and in both cases the Kabbalistic sense—i.e., "man's incapacity/non-reception/rejection of the Light"—is strikingly clear. It is needless to say that when it comes to Holy Writ, we are confronted, once again, not with dogmatic theology, but above all with a mystical knowledge of the divine. Let me add, with reference to your letter, that I have not as yet read St. John of the Cross and should do so, given what you have said.

Just as I was about to send to Bill Carroll a copy of my article, with the suggestion that I speak on that topic, I received the enclosed announcement concerning the conference, which precludes me from doing so. (You may be interested to note that the Archbishop of Lublin—a close friend of the Pope—is one of the participants.) However, I do intend to broach the subject of Kabbalah and Boehme informally: it does after all bear upon "Time, Creation, and Cosmology," the topic of the conference. In this way I can get a sense of how Catholic intellectuals are likely to react to the doctrine in question before presenting a lecture or submitting a paper on the subject. If the reaction turns out to be drastically negative, I may save myself the trouble! I am hopeful, however, that there will be some interest, some modest openness at least, to vistas of this kind.

My own major problem with Boehme has to do with his conception of the Holy Trinity. Boehme does of course accept the idea of the Trinity—even as he accepts all Biblical data—but his understanding or interpretation thereof differs sharply from the Catholic, which in fact it seems to contradict. Thus, in one of his comparatively rare references to the "*heilige Dreifaltigkeit*," Boehme tells us explicitly that the Son alone is a Person: "*Gott ist keine Person, als nur in Christo.*"[2] This of course is shocking to our Catholic sensibilities. What is more, it seems not even to accord with Biblical data: how can the Father, for instance, love the Son, if the Father is *not* a Person? Or how could Christ enjoin

---

[2] "God is not a person, save only in Christ."

upon His disciples to pray to *"our Father, who art in heaven"*? How can one address a non-person?

I surmise, however, that the problem lies with the concept of personhood, which apparently is not quite as simple and univocal as one normally thinks. It seems to me that the relation of the Father to the Son may prefigure the distinction between "subconscious" and "conscious" on the psychological plane, in which case it becomes clear that the Father cannot be a "person" in precisely the same sense as the Son. And let us recall that St. Thomas defines personhood abstractly in terms of "relation," which is to say that he relinquishes the ordinary "anthropomorphic" connotation of the term, presumably because the latter does not in fact apply to the Father and to the Holy Ghost. The point I am driving at is that Boehme's seemingly paradoxical and overtly "heretical" assertion could yet enshrine a valid and indeed fundamental theological insight.

I have often thought that there may be two kinds of so-called heresies: *intrinsic* and *extrinsic* one might say (a point, as I recall, made somewhere by Frithjof Schuon[3]). Now, an intrinsic heresy contradicts not only a dogmatic teaching of the Church, but truth itself: in a word, it is simply false—and surely there is no shortage of such. However, there seem also to be heresies of the extrinsic kind: teachings, namely, which contradict the "letter," so to speak, of this or that dogmatic affirmation, but are nonetheless expressive of a theological[4] truth. And as you can see, I am suggesting that the "heresies" of our Jacob Boehme are precisely of this latter kind. It seems to me, moreover, that even some of the well-known historical heresies against which the Church has fought may prove in the end to be "extrinsic." A case in point

---

[3] A highly influential 20th-century author of remarkable and at times exceedingly profound commentaries on the religions of the world, who needs however to be approached with caution by virtue of the fact that he misconceives Christianity.

[4] I am here using the term "theological" in a broad sense, transcending the distinction between a "theology" and a "theosophy."

would be the Nestorian Christology, given that Boehme's Christology is itself Nestorian (as Deghaye points out).

The question now presents itself: If such be the case, why did the Church struggle so hard to establish its own dogmatic position? Why fight, as it were, against truth? I think the answer is contained in a perennial recognition: the fact, namely, that not all knowledge is suitable for immature or unregenerate souls. As Deghaye observes: "*Die Erkenntnis reicht nur dem geläuterten Menschen zum Segen; für den unwiedergeborenen Menschen ist sie ein Gift.*"[5] Of course St. Paul has said much the same when he distinguishes between "milk" and "strong meat." I don't like to use the terms "exoteric" and "esoteric" because they have been so much misused; but the distinction needs ultimately to be made. What has happened in the Church, as I see it, is that an exoteric level of understanding has progressively stifled and eventually outlawed the esoteric: one wonders how many bona fide sages have in fact been burned at the stake! Certainly Boehme would not have fared too well, say, in 13th-century Spain. Now, one obviously has need of the exoteric—and in a sense every "church" *is* exoteric—but there is need as well for the leaven of the esoteric: for the unmitigated truth that "*shall set you free.*" And that is presumably "the mystical knowledge of the divine" which you contrast with rational (i.e., dogmatic) theology.

Permit me to add one more point. I don't know to what extent Vatican II can be seen as a reaffirmation of the esoteric; it strikes me rather as an exoterism run wild: an exoterism which turns against itself "from below." But be that as it may: in breaking down "the hard shell" of an exoterism that had become so to speak institutionalized, the Council has at least in principle opened the door to the esoteric. And that may, in the long run, prove to be a blessing after all: for it has been my conviction—ever since I learned what the word means—that only a bona fide revival of the authentically esoteric within the higher ecclesiastic

---

[5] "The [higher] knowledge benefits only the purified; for the un-reborn it is a poison."

ranks will enable the Church to prevail against the onslaught of the modern world. I know from all that you have so kindly communicated to me over the past months that you share this conviction—a fact which means much to me.

Getting back to the problem of introducing the Kabbalah or Boehme to a Catholic audience: I am wondering whether it may not be necessary to say more or less all that has been said above. It need not, of course, be put quite that way; but it seems to me that logic demands that we distinguish clearly between "the mystical knowledge of the divine" and rational or dogmatic theology (inclusive of Thomistic philosophy as it is commonly understood). To defuse the charge of "heresy" moreover, and open the door to an esoteric level of understanding, it is needful to point out the inherent limitation or relativity of rational dogmatic formulations *per se*—an exceedingly delicate point which, for a variety of reasons, may not go over too well, say with professors of theology! Now, quite frankly, I am fearful of what might happen if the attempt were made: perhaps it is foolish and intrinsically harmful to speak "in public" along these lines. But then again, the time may be at hand when some idea of the esoteric needs be disseminated within the Catholic intellectual ranks. Now, your kind letters and words of counsel have been an enormous support to me in that regard. But as you can see, I am quite confused and uncertain as to the "how" and "how much." And everything, of course, depends upon this!

Let this be all for today. And to tell the truth, I feel guilty for having already taken so much of your precious time.

Thea and I send our love and all good wishes for the New Year. May our Lord and Our Lady bestow upon you health and strength in abundance! And I have one other wish: may we have the good fortune of meeting you again in 1999, *Deo volente.*

Yours cordially,

Wolfgang

January 7, 1999

Dear Wolfgang,

Many many thanks for yours of December 30. Your conclusion about the accurate meaning of theosophy is very acceptable to my mind; and, precisely for the reason you give, theosophy is not coterminous—perhaps "not compatible" is as good a term— with theology. Yes, the root of the difference lies in the distinction between reason (human reason) and what shall we call it?— the intuitive, the mystical, the *facie ad faciem* contrasting with the *videmus nunc per speculum in aenigmate.* We really haven't got an apt term for it.

Maritain, in his *Sept Degrées du Savoir,* sometimes tries to establish what he called "metaphysical intuition"; his purpose was to rationally explain how, without the direct help of supernatural grace—therefore purely and simply on the natural plane—a person such as a poet or a composer or writer or artist could "perceive" (or "know" or "intuit") God. One of his examples was G. Manley Hopkins and his "inscape" explanation of his apparently direct (not rational) perception of God. I find Maritain's "metaphysical intuition" to be an unnecessary entity (as Thomas laid down: *"Entitates non sunt multiplicanda sine necessitate"*).

No doubt about it: no matter what name we choose, mystical theology (let's stipulate the use, just for verbal convenience) goes beyond rational or dogmatic theology. The "mere straw" of Aquinas reflects that.

Regarding Boehme and the Trinity: I don't find his *"Gott ist keine Person,"* for he immediately adds what for me is the key to his thought—*"als nur in Christo."*[6] Boehme can call Christ a person, but neither the Father nor the Holy Ghost; because, as you point out, in speaking of the three divine "persons" we must (dogmatically) define "person" as a relation, not at all anthropo-

---

[6] The first affirmation—"God is not a person"—is followed by a second: "except in Christ."

morphic. This is one corner of the Trinitarian theology that has been left untended and undeveloped. It has had dire consequences; several so-called heresies (early Nestorians and Assyrians/Chaldeans) lacked in their North-West Semitic languages any refined vocabulary to distinguish three important entities: person, individual, and nature. Their Greek (and Latin) translators in the early centuries had no technical knowledge of Syriac and Aramaic.

The only reason we humans (believers) can address God is, as you say, through Christ and in Christ, because He is the perfect anthropomorph through whom and in whom we can know, praise and adore the bodiless Father and the Spirit. As you point out, only the Son could become incarnate, could be an anthropomorph, because the Father cannot be generated (His "Personhood" is to generate), nor can the Holy Spirit become incarnate (His "Personhood" is to proceed as Love of the Father and Son). Only the *relational* consideration saves Christian believers from the cruel trap of a misapplied logic: the Trinity is kaput without the relational.

This, I personally think, is why the humanity (*sensu pleno*) of Christ—his perfect anthropomorph identity—is the key. The unbeliever trips over this claim. When Aldous Huxley was dealing with the ascetic excesses encouraged by Père Josephe (in Huxley's *Grey Eminence*), he had to blame the anthropomorphic identity of the "historical Jesus" for all these excesses, and go on to pontificate that this Christic anthropomorphism was what spoiled the divineness of Christianity in general and of Père Josephe with his Calvarian Nuns in particular.

Just a century before Père Josephe and his bloody master, Cardinal Richelieu, John of the Cross carefully delineated the path to mystical union with God (Father, Son and Holy Ghost) through the anthropomorph Jesus. But Huxley could not in any way understand the Darkness of ascending Mount Carmel. For me, the fatherhood of the Father is a relational thing, as is the identity of the Holy Spirit, as finally is my sonship under God. No doubt in my mind, we should inquire more into Boehme's thought and perception.

Your distinction of intrinsic and extrinsic heresies is admirable (and totally acceptable to this man). Unfortunately, Vatican II was, as you say, an exoterism run wild. But it may serve (at a later date) to facilitate the sense of the esoteric. In all this, Wolfgang, my overall judgment on our present forms of Christianity (those that matter: Roman Catholic, Protestant, Eastern Orthodox) is that as visible structures they are on their way out.

Please God, you will find a way of broaching this vital subject so as to start a dissemination of a healthy esoterism that leaves unchangeable dogma intact and enables the mind to be enriched by the greatness of God the Creator as "epiphanied" by the Baby and Mother. It's worth a try.

I have just received yours of January 2.[7] I have no doubt we can as dogmatically sound Catholics accept Boehme's position.

You hit the nail on the head when you concentrate on Person—the notion, the origin, the theological coloration given it by Catholic and Greek and Russian interpreters.

Your January 2 letter has gems. Absolutely, the Father is not a person in relation to us; He is that only *per Christum*. Boehme's *Ungrund* is surely a human way of saying what Christ—almost impatiently—said to Philip in response to his childish "Show us the Father, and that will be enough." The Gospel retort of Jesus is almost a shout: "*Don't you know? Who sees me sees the Father, Philip.*" Christ's mediation is capital. Otherwise, Wolfgang, we are lost in Hell, and all our preaching and believing is "*Schall und Rauch.*"[8]

I am sure our beautiful God will mirror to a new degree all that we have lost of old Vienna[9] and (for me) what I have lost of my Celtic language, countryside, and home culture.

Love to you and Thea, and Blessing

Malachi

---

[7] This letter has apparently been lost.
[8] Famous words of Goethe; literally: "sound and smoke."
[9] A reference evidently to my impressions of Vienna as related in my letter of November 18.

VIII

St. Catherine of Genoa and the Supernatural

St. Catherine of Genoa and the Supernatural

January 19, 1999

Dear Father Malachi,

Thank you most cordially for your beautiful letter of January 7, which I have read and re-read many times. I am not only pleased but relieved to find that you "have no doubt that we can, as dogmatically sound Catholics, accept Boehme's position." This is what I have been trying, for some time, to persuade myself of. Quite frankly, however, I needed your unequivocal assent to dispel the last remaining vestiges of doubt. To open one's soul to the theosophy of Jacob Boehme—that is not a small step after all.

I am intrigued by your observations regarding Jacques Maritain, all the more since I have had occasion not too long ago to acquaint myself in some degree with his views concerning "natural mysticism." To be sure, when it comes to the "mystical experience" of poets, composers, and artists, I too remain doubtful that Maritain has something important and "necessary" to contribute. What is more, I dislike the term "natural mysticism," which strikes me not only as condescending, but as contradictory to boot, given that mysticism is concerned, after all, with the quest of God. So too, as you well know, I don't share Maritain's conviction that a "supernatural" mysticism can exist solely within the visible confines of the Catholic Church.

That said, however, I would add that I have been profoundly impressed by Maritain's thought as it applies to the Oriental traditions. Without going into this question at length, permit me to indicate at least briefly what it is that strikes me as exceedingly profound. Vedantic doctrine, as one knows, insists that there is *in the final count* no difference between the individual self (*jivātma*) and the Supreme Self (*paramātma*), and that the realization of this identity or "non-duality" (*advaita*), attained on the highest level of mystical experience, constitutes what is termed *moksha* or Liberation: the Supreme Knowledge (*purna jñāna*), namely, that "*shall set you free.*" What the Hindu mystic of the highest rank realizes at the summit of his *sādhanā*, his spiritual quest, appears thus to conform to the *mahāvākya* or "great saying"—as ancient, it seems, as the snow-capped mountains guarding the high ground where it was first conceived—the laconic *tat tvam asi*, "that thou art."

Now, for a long time I have been troubled by the question whether this quintessentially Vedantic teaching is compatible with the Christian truth. I find it hard to see how, "as dogmatically sound Catholics," we can admit what this *mahāvākya* appears to signify. But then—whatever the Vedantic exegetes or "theologians" may have to say by way of interpretation—there remains the hard fact of *nirvikalpa samādhi*: that Himalayan summit of mystical experience which Hindu sages have scaled, again and again, since time immemorial—a fact which I, for one, cannot doubt for an instant! The question then becomes: can we, as Catholics, "situate" that Summit? Now, it seems that Maritain's thought sheds light on this, to me burning issue. What he proposes is the idea that states or degrees of knowing properly termed "*nirvanic*" may be viewed as an intuition of "*being*" in the sense of the Thomistic *esse*, the "act of being" which founds our existence and yet transcends *essence*, transcends even the genus of man. Concerning this realization Maritain writes: "But here we have an experience of God *in quantum infundens et profundens esse in rebus*,[1] directly attained in the mirror of the substantial *esse* of the soul. . . . God, without being Himself an object of possession, is attained by this same act of the experience of the self." He explains, moreover, how Hindu philosophers, lacking the resources of Thomistic ontology, could have confused "the two absolutes," and thus arrived at a formally erroneous conclusion. What is more, he opines—and I think, not without reason— that, in Hindu tradition, philosophy is not so much a "science," in our sense, as it is an adjunct of spiritual method. Thought becomes thus a means to direct experience. . . . Finally, let me say that the seminal ideas of Maritain on this subject have been developed, as you may know, by two disciples: the Indologist

[1] Freely translated: "insofar as He fills all things to their very depth."

94

Olivier Lacomb and the Islamic scholar Louis Gardet namely. After numerous publications of their own the two collaborated on a book entitled *L'Experience du Soi*, which appeared in 1981; needless to say, I plan to read it.

Someday, *Deo volente*, we can perhaps discuss this question, which, as you know, intrigues me greatly. Meanwhile, however, I try not to think too much about it; better to concentrate on other matters closer to my immediate religious, philosophical and scientific concerns: for instance, the doctrine of Boehme, which satisfies all three of these stipulations. You will recall, from my last paper, that it connects even with the physics of light: the subject of Lorentz invariance!

Regarding Boehme's conception of the Holy Trinity, our recent exchange has effectively removed my doubts. It remains to reflect upon his so-called "Nestorian" Christology in the hope of resolving that question as well. I was particularly interested in your remarks concerning "several so-called heresies"—which include the "early Nestorian"—to the effect that this issue has much to do with linguistic imprecisions: for instance, in translating from Syriac or Aramaic to Greek and Latin. I doubt not that these "linguistic" factors have contributed their share to the confusion surrounding the "Nestorian" question. In the case of Boehme's teachings, we are fortunate to have these in a language we know perfectly well.

Although I have not read Aldous Huxley's *Grey Eminence*, I can appreciate your observations relating to the limits of his understanding when it comes to the Christian position. It is strange that contemporary Western intellectuals seem to have a far greater affinity to the tenets of Oriental mysticism than to the teachings of Christianity! I still recall the impact of Huxley's *Perennial Philosophy* when I read the book almost half a century ago, convinced that this was indeed the last word. From how many grave errors—one right after the other—did my Good Angel graciously rescue me!

I am very pleased that you concur with the distinction between "intrinsic" and "extrinsic" heresy, as also with my cursory remarks regarding the need for an esoteric level of under-standing: "an esoterism," as you say, "that leaves unchangeable dogma intact." This, it seems to me, is indeed the crucial point: the mark of an *authentic* esoterism—even as Christ Himself came, not to "*destroy*," but precisely to "*fulfill*."

Finally, as you can well imagine, I was very much struck by your suggestion that the "visible forms" of Christianity—be they Catholic, Protestant, or Orthodox—may in fact be "on their way out." I do not pretend to understand with any degree of accuracy how you envisage this ongoing decline, a perception based doubtless upon a wealth of experience and observation in many pertinent domains, and on various levels. I can see that we are witnessing the accelerating corruption of Christian institutions, and above all, the Catholic Church: it is as if the animating spirit—which is ultimately the Holy Ghost—had withdrawn from its ecclesial forms, to be eventually replaced (as Our Lady had predicted at La Salette) by the foul breath of Antichrist him-self. One is forced to surmise, of course, that the papacy, the epis-copate, and the priesthood will remain, howbeit it in an outwardly diminished form. Conceivably the Church of the third millennium will, in certain respects, resemble the early Church, even that of the catacombs; and perhaps what will eventually unify Christians will not be primarily the explicated tenets of a dogmatic theology, but something more inward, more mystical, which in a way contains the dogmatic formulations of the past while yet transcending them. It will be a Church, I like to think, that is able to appreciate and honor the likes of a Ramakrishna or a Ramana Maharshi[2]—not to speak of Christian mystics such as our Jacob Boehme!—without compromising its own dogmatic stance or generating the least confusion among the faithful. A Church, in other words, that is in a way inclusive of all truth, in keeping with the venerable dictum: "*All truth, by whomsoever it is spoken, is spoken by the Holy Ghost*." And finally I ask myself:

---

[2] Perhaps the greatest among the sages of India in modern times.

could anything *less* than this be truly Catholic, fully and authentically *katholikos*?

Thea and I are wondering how your recovery is progressing. We hope and pray that you are well on the road to a full restoration of motor function. We trust that this is the case.

Thea joins me in sending our love and all good wishes. And thank you again most cordially for that beautiful letter!

Yours faithfully,

Wolfgang

January 23, 1999

My dear Wolfgang,

Many many thanks for yours of January 19. As always with your letters, I will have to read it attentively two or three more times before it all becomes clear to me. In the meantime, what an exciting horizon you have opened up for me in Jacob Boehme.

Over all this discussion (not merely the themes of your last letter) there is a pendant question I feel I should adduce at this point. A question I have had since my early twenties when I was forcefully introduced to metaphysics *and* to Johannine mysticism. It's not really a question—rather, for me, it is a fundamental mystery.

I can enunciate it very simply, in fact deceptively simply: the proper relationship in our minds of the supernatural and the natural. To state it like that is simplistic, but it is a way of introducing the question.

The question arises from the exigency (exercised by theology) that the supernatural (the *vita divina*) is totally alien to created nature at least in the fundamental fact that nature has no claim, no right, no means of obtaining the supernatural. Scripture and theology are clamorously clear and insistent about the absolute gratuitousness of the supernatural. I have nothing in my human nature, *qua tolis*, of the supernatural; nor have I, by any force or power of nature, any chance of obtaining the supernatural. If I do obtain it, it is a pure gift, it is totally unmerited, undeserved, totally gratuitous.

If I held otherwise, I would lapse into Pelagianism or Semi-Pelagianism. Caricaturing Pelagianism or Semi-Pelagianism [it is] as natural man saying to God: "Thanks for the offer, but no thanks; I can make it on my own."

Modern (and modernist-minded) theologians in the post-War period came up with a counter-argument based on the Thomistic and Aristotelian *act* and *potency* theory. Actually we do receive the supernatural when we are Baptized, Confirmed,

98

Ordained, Married, Confessed, Anointed with Oils. We do receive it. Therefore we must have a *potency* for the supernatural; *quidquid recipitur, ad modum recipientes recipitur.* Therefore built into my very human nature, there is a potency for the supernatural. And that potency cannot be a natural element, it must be supernatural because nothing natural can enable me to accept the supernatural.

The very modern doctrine about supernatural grace has found its fullest expression in the explicit theological teaching of Pope John Paul II, who has insisted all his pontificate that every human being at *conception* is united with Christ—long before Baptism, if ever he *is* baptized. The embryonic human being is already possessed by and in possession of the supernatural, of supernatural grace.

There is no way of reconciling this teaching with the dogmatic rulings of Trent and Vatican I—forgetting, for the moment, the constant insistence of the bimillenarian Church that our supernatural participation is *totally* gratuitous.

By the way, all the moderns (von Balthasar, Congar, Chenu, Küng, etc., etc.) have accepted the idea of a supernatural potency now embedded in the human nature of every conceived human being. And this question about the relationship (nature vis-à-vis supernature) is the capital one in the new ecumenism founded by John Paul and the World Council of Churches plus other church related organizations.

Anyway, this question for me is a capital one. It comes at me from unexpected quarters. I don't know if you have ever read the treatise on Purgatory by Catherine of Genoa. On this question her teaching is superb but very disturbing for the current ecumenical "short-cut" (because that's what it really is). And the Roman Magisterium will have to give us new directions, at a later date, about John Paul's teaching—once his papacy has been terminated and he has gone home to God.

The point of my adducing someone like Catherine of Genoa is merely to underline in constant tradition the understanding that for participation in the Trinity's life (the supernatural life), nature has to be (for all intents and purposes, as it were) so subli-mated beyond any natural level that God absorbs all. I will send you a copy of Catherine's *Fire of Love*. It's a short treatise; but once having read it, you will never again think about Purgatory as you have hitherto done, nor will you ever again think of our consummation in the Beatific Vision as you have hitherto.

If all this sounds "preachy," I didn't mean it like that. But today the big loss among former Christian populations is this sense of the supernatural, thereby offending priesthood, bishop-hood, religious orders, marriage, and the understanding of the Seven Sacraments.

Doubtless we will discuss this question. Doubtless, too, Boe-hme has some light—mystical light—to shed on the issue.

Please thank Thea for her beautiful card and the news of her work (so successful) with once-upon-a-time non-choristers who with her direction performed so musically and so inspiringly. A great lady!

Blessings on both of you, and Love

Malachi

January 24, 1999

Dear Wolfgang,

A short note to accompany this little essay of Catherine of Genoa.

The Leitmotif of her teaching seems to me to be the complete subordination of nature to the supernatural grace of God's life. Saints—mystics—use expressions like "annihilation," "death of the self" in order to say what happens when the soul is invaded by divine grace. The whole point of the soul passing through the Dark Night of Mount Carmel in John of the Cross's perspective is the "escape" from nature. I'm sure that there are parallels in Indian mysticism.

The only point I'm making with all this is that the idea of *point d'insertion* in the human soul for the advent of the supernatural, and a *point d'insertion* that is connatural to the soul—is constitutive of the soul *qua tolis* prior to any advent of supernatural grace—this idea I cannot see within the perspective of Roman Catholic traditional doctrine.

Apropos in general of Boehme, some of his more poignant expressions and language concern Lucifer and his fall from divine favor and grace. Any of the early Fathers from the second to the sixth century would echo the very same sentiments—even Origen.

In fine finali, I seem to find myself at the old traditional position, namely that the advent of supernatural grace into our souls is, indeed, an irruption, a brusque intervention into the natural order of human being. If I assume this, I seem to be able to explain all the epiphenomena.

Blessings,

Malachi

IX

From the Threshold

February 7, 1999

Dear Father Malachi,

How very good it was to speak with you the other day! We are delighted to learn of your good progress and state of recovery: that is wonderful news. Our conversation is still ringing in my ears, and I have been thinking about various points you have raised. Incidentally, I have ordered a copy of that fascinating book subtitled *On the Liturgical Consummation of Philosophy.*[1]

I am still in process of trying to understand the problematic of "nature versus the supernatural" which you have placed at the center of the contemporary theological debate. One evidently requires a sound familiarity with post-medieval Catholic theology to fully appreciate all that is involved—which puts me at a disadvantage. Yet, for whatever it may be worth, let me say that I find "the modern counterargument based on the Thomistic and Aristotelian *act* and *potency* theory"—as you have summarized it—to have, for me, the ring of truth. And is this doctrine not basically what St. Catherine of Genoa affirms when she says that God created the soul "with a certain beatific instinct towards Himself"? However, St. Catherine says more: for not only does the soul possess an innate potency "towards God"—an inborn tendency to participate in the Life of God—but this capacity, innate though it be, has been obstructed on account of Sin, Original as well as actual. Now, I am wondering whether the weakness and vulnerability of the "new theology" may not lie precisely in its tendency to skirt around the problem of Sin: to the modern mind the very concept is irksome in the extreme. Yet be that as it may, there is a vast difference, it seems to me, between acknowledging a potential for the supernatural and the doctrine apparently espoused by Pope John Paul II to the effect that every human being is—as it were "automatically"—united to Christ from the moment of conception. Is not this latter affirmation

---

[1] Catherine Pickstock's *After Writing* (Oxford: Blackwell, 1998).

clearly a case of confusing *potency* with *act*? And is it not also—and above all—a case of ignoring the reality of both Original and personal sin?

After I submitted my paper on "celestial corporeality" to *Sophia*, Seyyed Hossein Nasr, the editor, referred me to two treatises by Henri Corbin dealing with the metaphysics of Light and the Resurrection Body from the standpoint of Iranian Sufism. So I began to read these books—and became fascinated: what wonderful sages Iran has produced once upon a time! What especially fascinates me, as you can well appreciate, is their description of an ontological domain often termed "the Earth of Hūrqalyā," said to be "the place where spirit and body are one, the place where spirit, taking on a body, becomes the *caro spiritualis*, spiritual corporeality." And as Corbin points out with reference to these Iranian masters: "We might find their brothers in soul among those who have been called the Protestant *Spirituales*, such as Schwenckfeld, Boehme, the Berleburg circle, Oetinger, and others, whose line has been continued to the present day."

From the time of Zoroaster right up to the succession of Shi'ite masters, it seems, the sages of Iran have been meditating upon the theme of Light and Darkness; and I wonder whether the resultant metaphysics of light is not the most complete such doctrine enunciated anywhere. In any case, what I have been able to pick up thus far has revolutionized my thought on the subject of "celestial corporeality": even as a reading of St. Catherine of Genoa has "changed forever" how I think about Purgatory, so have these Iranian texts decisively impacted my conception of the *photeinos anthropos*, the "man of light" we are destined to become.

Permit me to give at least a few indications concerning this marvelous doctrine, which I am just beginning to assimilate. Concerning the colored photisms experienced "on the plane of Hūrqalyā," Corbin writes: "These lights, made into colors in the very act of becoming light, have to be represented as creating for themselves, out of their own life and nature, their form and their

space (that *spissitudo spiritualis*,[2] to borrow Henry More's
expression). These pure lights are, in the *act of light* which constitutes them, constitutive of their own theophanic form: actualize
the receptacles that render them visible. 'Light without matter'
means here a light whose act actualizes its own matter. In relation to the matter of the black body [by which Corbin understands the corporeality of our world], invested with the forces of
obscurity—with Ahrimanian darkness—it is no doubt equivalent to an immaterialization." Here lies the reason, I surmise,
why, in the spiritual world, extension is "intensive" (in Hamberger's sense).[3] In a word: where "spirit and body are one," how
can there be "mutually external parts"? The "geometrical" implications, however, of the Sufi doctrine need to be brought out by
way of a rather subtle analysis; and I don't know if that has been
done in the Iranian literature. A good question for Seyyed
Hossein Nasr!

Another point of capital importance is the fact that this
"Oriental theosophy" has been given an "existential" formulation
by a shaykh named Mollā Sadrā Shīrāzī (d. 1640), which seems to
complement the Thomistic doctrine in a remarkable way. Like
St. Thomas, Mollā Sadrā "gives the determinant metaphysical
preference to the act of existing, not to quiddity or essence."[4]
What I find the most striking, however, is that the Iranian master
perceives the act of existing as "the dimension of light of beings,"
whereas their quiddity is termed "their dimension of darkness."
What Mollā Sadrā has done, it seems to me, is to connect—with
a single masterstroke!—Thomistic ontology and Iranian (and
equally, Boehmian) theosophy: what a tremendous recognition!

[2] "Spiritual density"
[3] On the subject of "intensive extension"—which in my view is pivotal to an
understanding of "celestial corporeality"—see *Ancient Wisdom and Modern
Misconceptions*, pp. 84–89.
[4] In light of Catherine Pickstock's "Platonist" reading of Aquinas, however, it
is not a question of complementing but of *completing* the Thomistic doctrine
by bringing to light what might be termed its esoteric side. We shall have occasion to return to this major issue in the final chapter.

And incidentally: the doctrine accords beautifully with what Maritain has to say regarding the "intuition of being" attained by Oriental mystics at the culmination of their *sādhanā* (something I alluded to in my last letter).

I don't know if "excited" is the right adjective to describe my state of mind as I read Corbin's books, but it is the best I can come up with. I am not myself a mystic, as you know very well; but there are times, when I read (or write) about profound things, that I almost feel like one. Yes, *writing* too can have that effect! As Bernard Kelly, the English Thomist, once said: "Some of us pray best with pen in hand."

Permit me, in light of all this, to send you at least "*eine Kost-probe*" from one of Corbin's books. It is a section which deals with the notion of "black light," and connects profoundly, I surmise, with the doctrine of St. John of the Cross. And even though that section is taken from the middle of the book, and presupposes much of what has gone before, I think you will be able to read "above the lines" and extract its essence.

Perhaps I should mention that Seyyed Hossein Nasr collaborated for many years with Henri Corbin in bringing out critical editions of the Iranian theosophical literature (which at the time was practically unknown in the West). Due to his close association with the Shah of Iran he came to be viewed as *persona non grata* by the revolutionaries and barely escaped with his life—just in time, as it turned out, to deliver the 1981 Gifford Lectures in Edinburgh (the notes for which had been lost in the confusion of flight). Not too long thereafter Nasr was appointed Professor of Islamic Studies at George Washington University, and soon will be honored with a volume in the Library of Living Philosophers. I might add that I know of no other representative of *sophia perennis* and unrelenting critic of "the brave new world" who has received even the smallest fraction of such accolades from the contemporary academic world. Whatever the motive may be, one has in any case done well to honor such a man.

We think of you daily, and look forward to the great pleasure of seeing you, *Deo volente*, in August.

Thea joins me in sending our love and cordial greetings.

Yours faithfully,

Wolfgang

P.S. Corbin speaks with great respect of Goethe's *Farben-lehre*,[5] and points out that it connects perfectly with the Sufi metaphysics of light.

---

[5] A treatise on light and color which broke with the Newtonian theory and was, in Goethe's day, perceived to be the work of a dilettante.

April 22, 1999

Dear Father Malachi,

Let me begin by thanking you for the interesting article on René Guénon: it contains a good deal of material that is new to me. The author is no doubt right in objecting to Guénon's views regarding Christianity; but I am not sure that he is able to fathom and fully appreciate his contributions in other domains, especially to metaphysics and cosmology. As you know, I myself am greatly indebted to the French savant: practically all of my writing pertaining to ontology vis-à-vis science owes something to his clarifying influence.

The author of the article bases himself on a book by Marie-France James, entitled *Ésotérisme et Christianisme autour de René Guénon*, published 1981. It is interesting that he does not mention Borella's *Ésotérisme Guénonien et Mystère Chretien*, published in 1997, which strikes me as the definitive work on the subject. It is even more revealing that Borella nowhere mentions the earlier book (with which he must have been acquainted). I surmise he did not mention it because he perceives it to be slanted in its approach. What I especially value in Jean Borella, apart from his astounding depth, is his balance and impartiality. Notwithstanding the fact that he subjects Guénon's views on Christianity to a withering critique in the aforementioned treatise, he lets it be known that he nonetheless regards him as the greatest metaphysician of the twentieth century. I surmise, even so, that Guénon will remain forever controversial, viewed by some as a god and by others as a devil; and perhaps he was in truth a little of both! In any case, Guénon is someone who cannot be ignored. I am glad to see the article you have sent.

The conference at Cornell proved to be rewarding. Let me begin with Zycinski, the Archbishop of Lublin, a truly brilliant man (aged 51) who converses fluently in eight languages, yet is unpretentious, warm and affable. He said Mass for us every day, and his homilies were simple and charming: there was a sweetness in his voice. He is a shepherd who knows how to touch hearts. In daily encounters he loves to joke, and charms everyone with his quick and witty repartee. And yet, when the conversation turns serious, one finds oneself in the presence of a first-rate intellect, endowed with an astounding erudition. In a conversation with Professor Hodgson from Oxford, for instance, the Polish archbishop alluded with ease to English works of literature the Oxford don seemed not even to have heard of. Or again, when we had dinner at the house of Bill Carroll (the professor who organized the conference), I heard him engage in a spirited conversation, partly in French, with Cyrille Michon from the Sorbonne about some contemporary French philosopher few of us could place. At one point, while we were walking across campus, I mentioned to the archbishop the remarkable book by Catherine Pickstock: he was immediately interested, and remembered having heard something about this author in Washington on his way to Cornell. Later the same day he espied the book in Bill Carroll's library, and proceeded forthwith to read in it, oblivious of all that was going on around him. A few minutes later he concluded: "Oh, she writes beautifully!" I am sure it will not be long before he has read the entire book.

The morning I gave my lecture I handed him a reprint of my "Schrödinger's Cat" article, which he began immediately to scan. "I see you are interested in Whitehead," said he. So I explained in a few words in what respect I am indebted to that philosopher. "I too have been interested in Whitehead," was his response; "I have written two books on the subject." By that time I should have expected nothing less! After I gave my talk (the text of which I enclose), the Archbishop expressed his assent, and commended me warmly.

His own lecture on relativistic cosmology (the text of which I enclose as well) was impressive. I should add that Zycinski is well informed in these matters, and I recall someone saying that he holds a Ph.D. relating to that field (which again would not surprise me in the least). The prepared text, however, hardly conveys the full flavor of the presentation, which seemed quite extemporaneous, and was laced, here and there, with humorous remarks —as, for example, when the Archbishop from Krakow recalled how Yogi Berra, the baseball icon, when asked what time it is, responded with the question: "You mean, now?" I forget the particular point of relativistic cosmology this anecdote was meant to illustrate, but distinctly recall the delight of the audience.

What however puzzles me is this: not only is the Archbishop firmly committed to an evolutionist *Weltanschauung*, but what is more, he appears to be seriously interested in process theology (which doubtless accounts for the two books on Whitehead). I did not have a chance to talk with him on these issues—which perhaps is fortunate—and don't know therefore how irrevocable his evolutionist convictions might be, nor how committed he is to process theology. The mere fact, however, that he does have such an inclination strikes me as unfortunate.

Admittedly I have not studied process theology, and have in fact avoided the subject because I had found Whitehead's theological speculations (e.g., his chapter on "Religion and Science" in *Science and the Modern World*) quite unacceptable. I might add that this recognition did not strike me when I read the aforementioned book for the first time (at age fourteen, as it happens): only decades later, after becoming acquainted with René Guénon, and above all, with authentic Catholic theology, did I come to realize how upside-down these speculations really are. The fact alone that Whitehead stands outside the pale of tradition renders him unfit to speak to theological issues, no matter how brilliant he may be. As regards process theology, it strikes me from the outset as a theory which—like the Teilhardian— fails to grasp the fundamental and indeed elementary fact that God—"*with whom is no variableness, neither shadow of turning,*" as St. James apprises us—is by no means subject to time.

Getting back to the Archbishop: as we said goodbye I presented him with a copy of *The Quantum Enigma*, which he seemed pleased to receive. "I have heard very good things about this book. Would you inscribe a few words?" So I did, doing my best not to misspell his Polish name. And then I handed him also a copy of my Teilhard book, which seemed to please him less: the very title, after all, well-nigh gives the book away.[6] The chance is slim, therefore, that he will read it, let alone approve of what I have to say; and yet, when in the course of my lecture I stated that "whosoever takes seriously the word of Scripture must totally reject the evolutive interpretation of the Eschaton," the Archbishop seemed pleased. So perhaps there is hope after all. And if he does change his mind, what an impact this could have! There are rumors, as you no doubt know, that Zycinski is slated to be a Cardinal, and might even succeed Ratzinger.

I also met Peter Hodgson, the Oxford nuclear physicist with whom I had corresponded for some time. He was very affable, and we had some long and pleasant talks. As concerns the interpretation of physics, there is little chance that we can ever see eye to eye since he is deeply committed to an Einsteinian position. He believes that the wave function or state vector refers, not to a physical system (as the Copenhagen school maintains), but to a statistical ensemble. The individual systems themselves, moreover, are to be conceived in more or less classical terms. For example, a particle has a well-defined position and momentum, moves in accordance with deterministic laws, and in a word, exhibits no quantum strangeness. What causes strangeness, Hodgson believes, is the misconceived notion that the wave function gives a faithful description of individual systems. Now, for my part I concur with the majority of physicists to the effect that all is not well with the ensemble approach, that in fact it finally proves to be untenable. I have the suspicion, moreover, that Hodgson's predilection for an Einsteinian position derives from a commitment to the Cartesian ontology, as in the case of his friend Stanley Jaki. My own view, as you well know, is very much the opposite. I find that the standard Hilbert space approach to quantum theory (the von Neumann formulation) accords perfectly with the non-Cartesian and indeed Thomistic ontology I hold to be true. I see no reason, therefore, to search for a deterministic substratum

---

[6] *Teilhardism and the New Religion* in the original TAN Books edition.

beneath the quantum level, and am in fact persuaded on metaphysical grounds that no such substratum exists. As you will
recall, I perceive quantum indeterminacy to be a residual potency,
and thus an effect of *materia prima*, as I explain in my book.[7] I
find it amazing, moreover, that Catholic thinkers, of all people,
could subscribe to an ontology which reduces the universe to a
mechanism, a kind of gigantic clockwork.

Despite this fundamental disagreement, however, Hodgson
and I have had some very pleasant discussions, as I have said, and
have grown to respect each other. For my part, I admire Hodgson's aristocratic bearing and impeccable manners ("every inch
an Oxford don"), and above all, his deep and genuine Catholicism. I have seen him cradle his face in his hands after Holy Com-
munion. He now devotes himself almost exclusively to writing
and lecturing on the relations of science and theology, and has
recently become the president of an international association of
Catholic scientists (which conceivably I may join). Not long ago
he was invited by Archbishop Zycinski to lecture at Lublin. He
seems to know everyone. When I happened to mention something about Josef Pieper,[8] he said: "Yes, I met him in '92 at Inns-
bruck." Incidentally, I gave Hodgson too a copy of the Teilhard
book, with better results... We have agreed to meet again at
Oxford on September 20, an encounter to which I look forward.

So as not to swell this letter too much, let me break off the
account of the Cornell conference at this point. I could of course
ramble on for a few more pages, but the above does cover, I
believe, the major impressions. Suffice it to say that I returned
from the meeting stimulated and enriched. And yes: it appears
that what I had to say did touch a few hearts. The most precious
testimony (to me) came from an undergraduate, who confided
in a perfectly ingenuous manner that "the joy of Christ emanated

---

[7] *The Quantum Enigma.*
[8] A German philosopher gifted with a rare ability to bring inherently Thomistic doctrine alive and in fact render it captivating to a contemporary audience.

from you during your lecture"—to which I can only say: would that it were so!

It was good to speak with you prior to my departure, and a great comfort to receive your words of encouragement and priestly blessing. Thea joins me in sending you our love and warm regards.

Yours faithfully,

Wolfgang

May 19, 1999

Dear Father Malachi,

I have already had occasion to thank you for introducing me to Catherine Pickstock's wonderful book. As you can imagine, I am electrified by her conclusion that "the event of transubstantiation in the Eucharist is the condition of possibility for all human meaning"—an oracular pronouncement I dimly perceive to be true. I am reminded of Meister Eckhart's dictum: "Words derive their meaning from the Word," which seems to point in the same direction.

Not long ago, moreover, when I read Josef Pieper's little book, *Musse und Kult*, I was struck to find that this Catholic philosopher has arrived at a conclusion similar in certain respects to Catherine Pickstock's thesis, but from a different direction or point of view. He argues, first of all, that human culture—as embodied, for instance, in the *artes liberales*—is rooted in *Musse*, "leisure." Such, after all, is the original meaning of the word "*schola*" from which our *school* and *Schule* are derived. Having established this major insight (in the first half of the book), Pieper goes on to examine in depth the concept of "leisure." By way of a discourse which strikes me as masterful, he shows that authentic leisure rests upon Sacrifice, and indeed, upon Liturgy! A portion of space and time are taken out of the profane domain (the "*Arbeitstag*") and "given to God": all true human culture hinges upon this act. It is the source of all genuine nobility and true joy. One sees this, for instance, in the feasts—those outbursts of authentic joy to be found only within a traditional society—in which the performance of religious rites plays a foundational role. One knows that Plato in the *Laws* insisted upon such a foundation, as did Confucius in the *Analects*. Even the American Indians had their foundational rites. And in the Vedic civilization, of course, *yajña* was paramount, and applied to every sphere of life. Even the act of procreation was conceived in sacrificial terms: the offering of an oblation upon an altar of God. It was written that only thus could "Aryan offspring" be brought into the world. In sum, I surmise the post-Christian West may possibly be the first society in human history bereft of a liturgical foundation.

According to Pieper, then, human culture is rooted in liturgy: in the praise and worship of God. And this, to be sure, is the reason why, in our secularized Western civilization, culture in the true sense has declined to the point of disappearance, to be replaced by all manner of *Ersatz* which in the end only exacerbates the profane blight. What a time, incidentally, for segments within the Church to deny the sacrificial character of the Mass, to proclaim it to be simply "a meal"!

Getting back to Catherine Pickstock: I can understand why the restoration of metaphysics in this age needs to start with a refutation of Derridean post-modernism. For if indeed one were to affirm the discipline on any other basis, it would be instantly vulnerable to post-modernist attack. One could say that Catherine Pickstock has beaten Derrida at his own game, and in so doing has, as it were, "snatched the pearl of metaphysics from the dragon's jaws." I find it altogether fitting, moreover, that it was a woman who has accomplished this heroic deed: thus representing Her to whom it was given from the outset "*to crush the serpent's head.*"

I cannot therefore resist the temptation to say a few more words concerning Catherine Pickstock's truly marvelous book. I read it every morning; and the more I read, the more "the wonder grows." A few days ago it suddenly struck me that "celestial space"—on which I have pondered so much—is basically none other than "liturgical space," the "space of doxology" which our author delineates so magnificently in the chapter entitled—most appropriately!—"Seraphic Voices." This became clear to me when I read the following remarkable lines (beginning on p. 229): "So although God is not in a place because He is infinite, He is not non-spatial, for He situates sites themselves. And therefore He is the eminent (or pre-eminent) space of preoccupation, which gives space its job in advance of itself, which is to make space for worship."

"This radiant and excessive structure of divine space," she brilliantly goes on, "overflows into that of our liturgical journey, in such a way as to defamiliarize mundane topologies which, by defining space as pure extension, stipulate that the goal of a journey cannot be simultaneously attained and postponed, before and after, within and without, 'to hand' and distant. These apparently oxymoronic combinations are definitive of liturgical space…" What a flood of light this sheds on the subject of "celestial corporeality": on everything, in fact, that matters!

I trust you have received my long letter of April 22 in which I describe, among other things, my impressions of the astounding Archbishop Zycinski.

Thea joins me in sending you our warm regards and best wishes.

Yours faithfully,

Wolfgang

June 4, 1999

Dear Father Malachi,

It would be trite and altogether insufficient to say that I enjoyed our telephone conversation this morning! I must however admit that I can far more readily express what is in my mind than what is in my heart. But perhaps you know very well what I would say if only I were able.

At breakfast I conveyed your words of encouragement to Thea, which brought her great joy and comfort. "Join the club of sufferers"—these words touched her deeply. We need to hear this again and again, and we need to hear it from the lips of a holy priest speaking with the authority of Christ.

Much as I am by nature given to the theoretical domain, I realize that the most burning question pertains to the practical order: *Can you suffer?* Can you carry your Cross? Can you submit to Crucifixion? And I fear that if the answer be negative, all our words—no matter how sublime—amount to little more than "*Schall und Rauch.*" I have long understood that the saint who is not a philosopher is greater by far than the philosopher who is not a saint.

Let me pass on to you now a few quotations from Jacob Boehme—a philosopher-saint indeed!—which bear upon the specific points we touched upon.[9] They are taken from that lovely book by Julius Hamberger (*Die Lehre des Jakob Boehme*) a copy of which I sent you. Let me note, first of all, that chapter 14 (pp. 214–230) dealing with sacramental theology seems to convey insights of the highest interest (to me at least). While acknowledging all that the Church has taught, it appears to transcend the exoteric point of view, if I may put it so.

But now to Boehme himself. With regard to the "innate supernatural in man" he has this to say: "As soon as a child has received life in his mother's womb there glimmers in him out of

---

[9] This refers to a telephone conversation we had that morning.

his first origin a celestial or hellish nature [the original term, *Wesenheit,* admits of no easy translation]."[10] I am of course struck by the fact that Boehme too speaks of "first origins"—but even more so by the fact that he distinguishes two kinds of "supernatural" endowments: a celestial and an infernal namely. I don't think Boehme would quite agree with our present Pope! One may surmise that what Boehme is saying here needs to be interpreted in light of what he teaches in regard to the "*Gnaden-wahl,*" the vexed question of "predestination" to which he devoted an entire book (his last, as I recall).

With regard to the Sacraments and the question of their necessity, the following two passages strike me as being of paramount significance:

> We should not be exclusively devoted and concerned with only those means, that the Flesh and Blood of Christ be partaken solely in the form of bread and wine as the understanding of our time mistakenly maintains. It is the Faith, rather, that eateth and drinketh ever the Flesh and Blood of Christ if it hungers for God's love and mercy, whether by means of the blessed Food, or without these means.

> Reason declares: Because Christ says that whosoever does not eat the flesh of the Son of man does not have life in him; and because the Jews, Turks and ignorant heathen have no taste for such a food, they must all be damned. What blindness! The Turks, Jews and foreign nations whose desire and prayer is directed to the one God have indeed a mouth [for the divine Food], just not as a true Christian does. As is the desire or the mouth, so too is their food; they thirst for the Spirit of God, and so their partaking is of the kind it was before the human birth of Christ.[11]

[10] Translated from op. cit., p. 209.
[11] Op. cit., p. 209.

I would point out that Boehme seems to distinguish here between two Eucharistic modes: the reception of Christ *"vor und nach seiner Menschwerdung"*: "before and after his Incarnation." And this seems to connect with the Apocalyptic allusion to *"the lamb that was slain from the foundation of the world."* I venture to surmise that it may be the "flesh and blood" of the latter that is offered as spiritual food to the unbaptized "of pure heart."[12]

I will close now, so that I can get this letter off today. I would only add one thing: Thank you, dear Father Malachi, for being indeed my spiritual father, with all that this implies.

Thea joins me in sending you our love and all good wishes.

Yours faithfully,

Wolfgang

---

[12] For more on the question of "pre-Christian religion" I refer the reader especially to pp. 208–213 in Hamberger's book.

June 6, 1999

My dear Wolfgang,

One other remaining aspect of my conceptual difficulty about the natural/supernatural pairing concerns the gratuitousness (clumsy word) of the supernatural. And that is a given datum of Revelation: I can never have even the faintest claim on the supernatural. In order to be just human, I don't need it. Nor do I deserve it. Nor can I win it. Supernatural life by means of what tradition and Revelation call sanctifying grace (real—ontological—participation in God's divine life) is the sheerest of gifts.

I realize that if, as I know by experience and the infallible voice of the Magisterium Romanum, I have received this sheerest gift, then I must as a human nature have had a potency for the gift. But in strict logic that potency cannot be a mere nature: *quisquid recipitur ad modum recipientis recipitur*; the potency must be supernatural. And there I am with my dilemma—and threatened by, among other things, Pelagianism or at least semi-Pelagianism. And it doesn't help me off the horns of this nasty dilemma to say that the omnipotent and loving God creates the potency in me prior (ontologically but not temporally) to the infusion of the supernatural life. For that introduces into the dilemma of the ever-receding endless recession.

It is not very fair to obtrude our communication with this chestnut. But all my adult life I have had a fear of presuming about the access of the precious supernatural—without which I should join three quarters of my fellow-Americans in lamenting that Charismatic a few lengths from winning the coveted Triple Crown yesterday cracked the cannon bone and fractured the sesamoid behind it, and lost. With my supernatural optic, I can glance at my concomitant Angels quizzically while murmuring with that ancient virgin, Virgil: *sunt lacrimae rerum et mentem*

122

mortalia tangunt.[13] By the way, his nickname among his contemporaries *was* Virgil the Virgin.

I realize my problem is not to be resolved in a day. And it may be settled as Teresa of Avila solved the gnawing problem of predestination (the solution was *totaliter aliter*, she announced). And I can wait in relative tranquility until I am *facies ad faciem.* But while *in via* it would be nice to have clarity in a question which stands behind much of the open apostasy now stalking high and low in the Church of Christ.

Consolatory and godly kisses to Thea who towers over those dreadful pigmies who cannot even begin to understand her and what she signifies.

Blessings,

Malachi

---

[13] A haunting line from the *Aeneid* (Bk. I, line 462) referring to the "tears" evoked by "mortal things" in virtue (as one may presume) of their mortality.

X

Catherine Pickstock's
Esoteric Thomism

June 12, 1999

Dear Father Malachi,

As always, I was delighted to hear from you. I must admit that I don't understand the conceptual difficulty you cite relating to the natural/supernatural dichotomy: I mean, not in depth, as you do. It is presumably out of ignorance, therefore, that I offer the following thoughts.

The idea of "nature" entails that of "substance," and thus of the substance/accident dichotomy. Yet, on reading Catherine Pickstock's book, one comes to sense that these Aristotelian categories are not quite as absolute as we have tended to think. As she observes, Aquinas, in his doctrine of transubstantiation, has "stretched these categories to breaking point." What permits this "stretching" is the Thomistic *esse*: it is this conception that radically transforms the Aristotelian doctrine—transforms it, one might say, into a *Christian* ontology. Catherine Pickstock elucidates this radical transformation in responding to P. J. Fitz-Patrick's charge that Aquinas' doctrine of transubstantiation is incompatible with his overall ontology:

> However, this is only because FitzPatrick restricts the Thomist ontology to the form/matter, substance/accident level, taking no account of the Neoplatonistically-derived *esse/essentia* level which is capable of disturbing the prior categories.... Within this level of consideration, Aquinas shows that for every creature such an interval between *esse* and *essentia* exists and is constitutive of its reality.... Hence every creature is "pulled" by its participation in *esse* beyond its own peculiar essence—it exceeds itself by receiving existence—and no created "substance" is truly substantial, truly self-sufficient, absolutely stable or self-sustaining. It follows that the violation of the substance/accident contrast and the gap between *esse* and essence in the case of transubstantiation is only an extreme case of what, for Aquinas, always applies. All substances are "acci-

dents" in contrast to divinity, and become signs which, in their essence, realize a repetition and revelation of the divine "substance." (pp. 260–61)

Now, if transubstantiation appears, on an Aristotelian basis, as "an unnecessary, arbitrary, and scarcely comprehensible miracle" (as Catherine Pickstock charges), might not the same be said concerning the infusion of sanctifying grace?

The problem with the natural/supernatural dichotomy seems to lie with the first term, which presupposes individual substance. I have long been wary of this latter notion—which the Vedanta, for instance, rejects apodictically—and have come to believe that neither Plato nor Aquinas conceived of substance in absolute terms. To put it in Catherine Pickstock's idiom, they did not subscribe to an *immanentist* ontology. All discourse on "substances," in Aquinas no less that in Plato, is invariably dialectical, which is to say that the notion is accorded a merely provisional validity. As she observes, the distinction between *esse* and *essentia* "is capable of disturbing the prior categories." She means of course that the distinction does "disturb the prior categories," whether this fact is recognized or not. And for the most part, to be sure, it is not—which no doubt accounts for a host of seeming paradoxes, along with spurious resolutions thereof.

You speak of the supernatural life as "the sheerest of gifts." I would only add that the Thomistic ontology casts creaturely being itself in the category of gift. In fact, according to Catherine Pickstock's rendering, a gift that is not in fact a *given* but a *giving*, and as such is never severed from the transcendent donor. In a word, *being* is in a sense relational and open. All beings, moreover, by virtue of their participation in *esse*, are in a sense oriented towards God; where, then, is there actually room for the "merely natural"?

Our true nature, it appears, is defined by our eternal relation with God. The supposition that we have a natural being, to which something supernatural may or may not be added, is therefore misconceived. Of course, on a certain level we are obliged to think in such terms, and perhaps even Aquinas does so on occasion; yet in any case he transcends this supposition in the contemplation of *esse*, the key notion which does indeed "disturb the prior categories." What becomes of the "merely natural," I ask, once we realize, with Catherine Pickstock, that "the creature constantly becomes more itself precisely because of its contemporaneity with existence, since it is really distinct from its own being, which is not fully its own but is always re-arriving, always being regiven" (p. 129). The criterion of the "fully human" is therefore, quite simply, to be *open* to the ("supernatural"!) gift, which implies that *nothing is actually more natural to man than the supernatural*—even though the latter remains ever, as you say, "the sheerest gift."

I offer these thoughts to you for whatever they may be worth. As you can see, I am spellbound by what John Milbank of Cambridge calls "this supremely important book." Catherine Pickstock has instituted, I believe, a new and indeed genuinely esoteric reading of both Plato and Aquinas, and as Milbank observes, "enunciates a wholly new, wholly orthodox theology." God and His angels be praised!

Thea was thrilled with your gracious and indeed most consolatory words, which she will henceforth treasure and apply. She joins me in sending our love and warm regards.

With every good wish, yours faithfully,

Wolfgang

Postscript

Postscript

WITH MY LETTER of June 12, 1999, the correspondence with Malachi Martin comes to an end: on July 27 our beloved friend and spiritual guide departed from this world.

Looking back now upon this exchange, this sharing of thought and convictions, one central topic stands out and in a way takes precedence over all other subjects touched upon: to wit, the relation of "the natural" to "the supernatural." Again and again Malachi Martin returns to this issue to emphasize the "utter gratuitousness" of the supernatural, the fact that nothing in our nature entitles us to its reception, or even renders such a receiving possible. But the question remains: what *is* that "nature" beyond the pale of the supernatural, unreceptive even to its touch? Now this is where a "healthy esoterism," and in particular, the epochal discoveries of Catherine Pickstock come into play, "disturbing prior categories," starting with the "the natural" itself. The salient recognition definitive of this newly uncovered Thomism is the existence, for every creature, of "an interval between *esse* and *essentia*" that proves moreover to be "constitutive of its reality"—which is just what our common-sense conception of "the natural" denies. What this means in plain terms with reference to "the natural" thus conceived is what in fact every bona fide esoterism affirms: i.e., that in truth there *is* no such thing! The supernatural—if one may still use that term—proves thus to be ubiquitous, penetrating all spaces and not only founding the very existence of all existing things, but exerting *qua esse* an influence upon every creature, a "pull" as Catherine Pickstock says.

All of this, of course, is inherently incomprehensible on the level of ordinary "unschooled" thought, which is to say that the new *Weltanschauung* does not instantly destroy or even so much as dent our normal outlook. For the *viator*, now as before, "mountains are mountains and clouds are clouds," as the Zen master assures us, and all the accustomed conceptions remain *de facto* "undisturbed" after all. Nonetheless, for those who have—for an instant even—grasped the point, something momentous has taken place: in the uppermost reaches of their being a break-through has occurred, a threshold has been crossed. Something

133

hitherto undreamed of has come—instantaneously!—into par-
tial view, opening vistas which manifestly exceed the confines of
this, our "narrow world." What stands at issue, let us note, is an
intuition, or a level of knowing, that may properly be termed
"esoteric." The word should not disturb us: if there be such a
thing as St. Bonaventure's *"itinerarium mentis in Deum,"* then
even as every ladder has a highest rung, there must likewise be
something answering to that designation: i.e., a kind or degree of
knowing commensurate with the threshold of what Meister Eckhart termed "the breaking through." The fact is that every integral sapiential tradition has perforce its esoteric core, hidden
though it may be.[1]

Getting back to my unanswered letter of June 12: to
Thomism thus, as conceived in light of Catherine Pickstock's
magnum opus, which appears to have recovered the fullness of
the Thomistic legacy by unearthing its long-neglected *esoteric*
component. Now, this incomparably enlarged understanding of
what, prior to Vatican II, had been in effect the official philosophy of the Catholic Church, is what I wished to convey to Malachi Martin, to confront him with as it were: for it seemed that the
newly-opened vistas flatly contradict the hard and fast "natural/
supernatural" dichotomy upon which Fr. Martin appeared to
place so much weight. Encouraged by the fact that he had
evinced a conspicuously sympathetic interest in Catherine Pickstock's book, and playing the role of a devil's advocate if you will,
I presented him thus with a counter-argument, eager to learn his
response. But alas, the letter arrived too late; and whereas, most
assuredly, I cannot speak for Malachi Martin himself, it now falls
upon me to respond to the question posed as best I can.

What stands at issue is the fact that the concept of "the natural" which Fr. Martin opposes adamantly to the supernatural has

---

[1] That "esoteric core," moreover, is none other than *doctrinal gnosis*, the very
conception of which has been all but lost in modern times. On the relation of
doctrinal gnosis to dogmatic theology, I refer to the Postscript in *Christian
Gnosis*.

been "disturbed" by Catherine Pickstock's revelations to the point of invalidity, and that the aforementioned opposition has consequently been, in principle, resolved. But what precisely does this entail? Must we conclude that Malachi Martin's abiding concern—his repeatedly expressed insistence upon the categorical "otherness" of the supernatural in relation to the assumed "naturality" of the natural—was in fact misconceived? Now, if we were pure disembodied spirits, this might perhaps be the case; but obviously we are not. And that is precisely why Fr. Martin's admonitions have import after all, and why they prove in fact to be of imperative significance. These declarations speak to what may be termed our "existential" condition, and refer to what is ultimately the single most decisive issue; for they teach us to seek God the only way He can be attained: *"with all thy heart, with all thy mind, and with all thy strength,"* in a spirit of complete and unconditional submission. But then, if such an ontological humility is called for as an adjunct of Salvation, it follows that the nonexistence of the commonsense "natural" as a bona fide category does not invalidate Malachi Martin's abiding concern in the least, nor diminish its overriding urgency by one iota.

Meanwhile we need to remember that we are living in a post-Vatican II era of rampant apostasy, based in large measure upon a false and indeed *inverted* conception of the natural/supernatural polarity. These heretical notions have taken various forms, epitomized arguably by the theistic evolutionism of Teilhard de Chardin, whom I would identify as the arch-heretic, the veritable Arius of our age.[2] What Teilhard has done, basically, is to rotate the "vertical axis" of authentic metaphysics by ninety degrees, as it were, to coincide with the axis of time: the "above" has thus been transformed into futurity, thus turning the veritable Eschaton into his stipulated Point Omega. And in this flattened

---

[2] On this subject I refer the reader to my monograph *Theistic Evolution: the Teilhardian Heresy*, a book of which Malachi Martin approved: "You have made a very important and heterodox thinker as intelligible as his mental aberrations and loss of faith allow," he wrote on a postcard.

and indeed decapitated universe, this world without an "above," the perennial conception of the supernatural—to the extent that one can still conceive of a *super*-natural at all—becomes altered to the point of inversion. Instead of "descending," as mankind had always believed, the supernatural is now constrained to "ascend": to evolve out of the dust and slime of a primordial universe. Now Malachi Martin was of course acutely aware of these modernist fantasies; he had after all imbibed theories of this kind since his early Jesuit days at Louvain. And when—after seventeen years of hard endeavor![3]—he entered into the fullness of his maturity, he had become keenly perceptive of the spiritual poison that emanates invariably from such an inverted conception of the natural/supernatural polarity. Is it any wonder that for the rest of his life Malachi Martin insisted upon the absolute and unconditioned primacy of the supernatural? As he tells us explicitly in his last letter, dated June 6, 1999, it is the failure on the part of theologians to grasp this very point that "stands behind much of the open apostasy now stalking high and low in the Church of Christ."

One must not on that account imagine, however, that Malachi Martin was incapable of transcending the bounds of an inherently exoteric ontology: nothing could in fact be further from the truth. Let us be clear on this issue: a staunch Catholic who yet believes that a Lutheran mystic has "Christianized the ancient Hermetic wisdom, the pre-Christian Christological knowledge," does not, most assuredly, fit that description! In sharp contrast to theologians on either side of the current divide, Malachi Martin was keenly cognizant of an authentic esoterism manifesting itself under many forms and guises, which in fact he extolled as "the mystical knowledge of the divine as distinct from the rational," and was also moreover well aware of the pivotal fact that this dichotomy limits the reach of theology *per se* categorically.

This brings us to another objection—in a way the opposite of the preceding—sure to be raised by an appreciable number of

---

[3] He states so explicitly in a letter to Mary Martinez, a former Vatican correspondent, a copy of which came into my hands.

Catholics to whom the idea of a "pre-Christian Christological knowledge" as envisaged by Malachi Martin is anathema. Let it be duly noted, therefore, that the tenet of a pre-Christian revelation of Christ beyond the Judaic sphere has in fact been affirmed by saints and doctors of the Church, beginning perhaps with St. Justin Martyr, who referred to Christ as "the Word of whom every race of men were partakers," and declared that "those who lived according to this Word are Christians . . . as, among the Greeks, Socrates and Heraclitus."[4] One should add that Clement of Alexandria and his disciple Origen not only concur on this point, but clarify the issue by attributing such pre-Christian manifestations of the Logos to angelic revelations providentially dispensed to the various branches of mankind following their dispersion.[5] So too St. Irenaeus tells us that "The Word was ever present to the human race before He united Himself with His creature and was born in the flesh."[6] One might add that St. Augustine—inspired conceivably by this very dictum—has in fact *overstated* the case when he asserts that "The very thing that is now called the Christian religion was not wanting among the ancients from the beginning of the human race, until Christ came in the flesh, following which the true religion, which had already existed, was called Christian."[7] But be that as it may, we have perhaps said enough to indicate that the notion of a pre-Christian mode of Christianity is not quite as outlandish as many incline to think. In short, I submit that there exist (or have existed) what may properly be termed "*Logos* religions," and that there exists also a Patristic ecumenism of unquestionable orthodoxy affirmative of this fact. And I would argue moreover that this Patristic doctrine is urgently needed in our day as the ortho-

---

[4] *Apol.* XI, 6.
[5] Origen, *De Principis* III, 3.2.
[6] *Adv. Haer.* III, 16.5.
[7] Though this statement occurs in the *Retractiones* (I, 12.3), it is not one that he retracts.

dox antidote to the current post-Vatican II ecumenism, which I deem to be as ill-conceived as it is disastrous to the Church.

Let me recall, finally, that Malachi Martin concurs with my overall assessment of Vatican II; as he wrote in answer to the letter in which I made known my views on that subject: "Unfortunately, Vatican II was, as you say, an exoterism run wild. But it may (at a later date) facilitate the sense of the esoteric."[8] What he appears to be saying is that the ill-fated Council too has a function, a role to play in the ultimate perfection of the Church: and that is "to facilitate the sense of the esoteric." There are two implications here: first, that this "sense of the esoteric" was somehow stifled—or perhaps even proscribed—in the pre-Conciliar Church; and the second that "the esoteric" needs eventually to be re-admitted and valued for what it is. To be sure, nowhere does he say that explicitly. Yet, even so, I have no doubt that Malachi Martin regarded what he termed "a healthy esoterism that leaves unchangeable dogma intact" to be a *sine qua non* for the restitution of the Church: it seems to me that nothing short of this belief or certitude could explain his welcoming and indeed enthusiastic response to the various nuggets of bona fide esoterism—culled from both Western and Oriental sources—I cast his way, and account, in particular, for Malachi Martin's fascination with Jacob Boehme: the fact that he could speak of this ostensibly non-Catholic mystic as "a very Holy Spirit-enlightened man destined by Christ the Revelator of God's mystery to indicate to us of the latter days… how we can fill out our understanding of God," going so far as to suggest that "these refreshing insights" could serve to "deblock the impasse in which Roman Catholic intellectualism has been trapped these many years."

It is my earnest hope that the Malachi Martin letters here offered—these reflections by an exceedingly wise and holy priest—may contribute their share to "deblock the impasse," and by the grace of God may help seekers at this critical time of wellnigh universal "disorientation" to discern the Way and the Truth.

---

[8] See his letter of January 7, 1999 (chapter 7).

Malachi Martin:
A Brief Biography

MALACHI BRENDAN MARTIN was born on July 23, 1921, in County Kerry, Ireland. His father, a physician, was an Englishman by birth; yet the family was deeply Irish in its culture, and devoutly Catholic. After attending University College in Dublin for three years, where he majored in philosophy, Malachi Martin entered the Society of Jesus in 1939: as he averred near the end of his life, Pater Sanctus Ignatius had "captured my soul entirely." His entry into the Jesuit order marked at the same time the commencement of a life-long discipline that would eventually transform this fully "captured" novice into one of the most erudite scholars of his generation.

After completing a doctorate in archaeology, Oriental studies and Semitic languages at the Catholic University of Louvain, Malachi Martin pursued post-graduate studies at Oxford and the Hebrew University of Jerusalem, dealing in fact with what, in his letters, he refers to as a "pre-Christian Christological knowledge." Availing himself of Hebrew and Arabic sources predating the Christian era, he deciphered vestiges of that "Christological" wisdom and pondered its significance. As an expert, moreover, in the field of Semitic paleography, he published 24 articles on that subject alone. In addition, Malachi Martin contributed to the spate of research centered at the time upon the recently discovered Dead Sea Scrolls, a subject on which he wrote a two-volume book.[1] One should add that these studies took him from libraries into the field: to venerable archeological sites scattered over the Mediterranean world—an experience which doubtless left its mark upon his sensitive soul.

---

[1] *The Scribal Character of the Dead Sea Scrolls* (Publications Universitaires, Louvain, 1958).

Malachi Martin was ordained in 1954—fifteen years after entering the Jesuit order—and four years later assumed the coveted position of private secretary to Cardinal Bea, which he occupied till 1964. At one stroke Fr. Martin had now become a Vatican insider: a confidant to Cardinals, with direct access even to the Pope. And this leap, let us note, took place in 1958: the year of the fateful transition from the reign of Pope Pius XII to that of John XXIII. In conjunction with this advancement Malachi Martin was appointed to a professorship at the Pontifical Biblical Institute, where he lectured in various subjects, from Scripture to Hebrew, Aramaic and paleography. In addition he now taught theology at a branch of Loyola University, became associated with Orthodox and Oriental Churches, and was active in the Secretariat for Promoting Christian Unity, of which Cardinal Bea was the head.

But all was not well. Admittedly Malachi Martin, in his student days at Louvain, may have been partly sympathetic to avant-garde notions propounded by theologians such as de Lubac, Chenu, and Congar, who as he tells us himself were "privately" teaching doctrines which at the time were considered "dangerous" if not indeed heretical. But as the years went by he changed; and whereas the Jesuit order, and to a lesser degree, the Church at large during the heady days of Vatican II was shifting visibly to the left, Malachi Martin seems to have moved in the opposite direction: to the point of eventually embracing the unmitigated bimillenary tradition which had been affirmed unequivocally by the Catholic Magisterium up to that point in time. It thus came about that this highly favored Jesuit found himself, ever more urgently, confronted by a desperate dilemma: remain where he was and compromise his deepest beliefs, or give up all that he had gained by way of promotion: cast it all off as "mere straw." And as we know, Fr. Martin eventually chose the latter course. In June of 1964—only four months after he had accompanied Pope Paul VI on a pilgrimage to the Holy Land—he resigned his position at the Pontifical Institute, and in February of the following year asked to be released from the Jesuit order.

The request was granted, and in July of 1965 Malachi Martin broke his ties and departed from Rome. Despite various rumors to the contrary, we know both from his own testimony and that of his superiors that he left in good standing, and even with the blessings of Pope Paul VI, who sent him on his way with an appropriate dispensation. The following year he established residence in New York, where Cardinal Terence Cooke granted him permission to exercise the ministry of a secular priest.

Following his exodus from Rome and the Jesuit order, Malachi Martin found himself alone and without means in a radically new environment, a world drastically different from all he had known in the past. It was not easy. He needed first of all to support himself, and there was no one to help, no one to sponsor him. One wonders whether, in that bustling metropolis he had chosen henceforth to be his home, he could at the time count even a single friend. To make ends meet he took whatever work presented itself: from washing dishes to driving a taxicab. Yet he was at the same time making his presence known in the educated world, and by 1967, just a year after his arrival in New York, he became the recipient of a Guggenheim Fellowship which enabled him to embark upon his new career: that, ultimately, of a best-selling American author. The resultant first book, entitled *The Encounter: Religion in Crisis*, published in 1969, proved successful enough to win him the Choice Book Award sponsored by the American Library Association. The same year Malachi Martin received a second Guggenheim Fellowship, which allowed him to continue his literary labors without a break. *The Encounter* was followed by *Three Popes and the Cardinal* (1972), *Jesus Now* (1973), and the first of his four bestsellers, *Hostage to the Devil: The Possession and Exorcism of Three Living Americans* (1975). Apart from having been discovered as an engaging and rather colorful celebrity, Malachi Martin became at this time widely recognized as a leading scholar in various fields. Besides serving as an editor for the *Encyclopedia Britannica* and *National Review* he was sought after for interviews and as a guest on radio and television. Meanwhile he continued to write without a break, adding fourteen more major titles. The list ends with the 1996 publication of what is perhaps his *magnum opus*: *The Windswept House*.

Getting back to the '70s, it is to be noted that Malachi Martin's "swing to the right" had not yet reached its term: one needs but to read *Three Popes and the Cardinal*, for instance, to discover that as a work of historical commentary it yet bears traces of a liberal slant. A happy fault, as one can see in retrospect! For it is quite inconceivable that the Malachi Martin of the 90's would have become the recipient of a Guggenheim Fellowship, not to speak of the subsequent support he received from various quarters that helped significantly to propel his literary career. One wonders, for instance, how Malachi Martin might have fared had his first book borne the subtitle of his last, to wit: *How the Institutional Roman Catholic Church became a Creature of the New World Order!*[2] Having once attained the status of a bestselling author and literary icon, on the other hand, he could no longer be stopped; all the ideological left could then do was smear his name: and that certain individuals and groups proceeded forthwith to accomplish—in spades!

No one need be surprised; Malachi Martin had, after all, ruffled feathers in very high places: think of *Vatican: A Novel*, published by Harper & Row in 1986, in which he let it be known that Pope John Paul I had in fact been murdered, and pointed the finger at Cardinal Jean-Marie Villot, the former Secretary of State! Or perhaps even more to the point: his no-less-incendiary 1987 non-fiction bestseller subtitled *The Society of Jesus and the Betrayal of the Roman Catholic Church*. I see no need to recall the various and sundry allegations leveled against the former Jesuit from diverse quarters, nor cite the third-party literature that has subsequently arisen in his defense. I would rather quote the essential of what Malachi Martin himself has to say on the subject in a letter to a friend, a copy of which he sent my way. The "basic

---

[2] Despite the existence of copious notes, it appears the manuscript was never completed.

lesson," he writes, is "not allow myself to be diverted from fulfilling my mission as a priest and a servant of the Holy See of Peter." And he goes on to relate that, over twenty-five years ago, "I wrote to my Superior in Rome complaining about a recrudescence of these attacks, and suggesting a certain course of action. He wrote back quoting that passage from John's Gospel where Christ warns His disciples that the time will come when they would be ostracized and persecuted by people who would do that to them and think they were doing God's will. Can't you suffer, too, for Christ's sake? That was my Superior's answer." Yet even so the question remains why Malachi Martin should not have responded, should not have argued his case, as in fact St. Ignatius Loyola did himself when he was falsely accused of scandalous behavior. The answer, it seems, is that in our media-dominated world conditions have drastically changed: "These abusers and calumniators are not out to get the truth, to build up, to edify. Their bent is to destroy, to liquidate. . . . Hence, I found there was no point in even trying to communicate with them; everything they learned became merely grist for their grindstone of hate." I think we too may leave it at that.

It behooves us rather to understand, as clearly as we can, how Malachi Martin viewed the Church and the world, and what precisely he was missioned to accomplish. And the beauty is that he tells us so himself, as distinctly and explicitly as one could wish. He does so principally in eight interviews with the Canadian journalist Bernard Janzen, conducted in the final decade of his life: here, in these definitive disclosures, he shares with us the vision of the Catholic Church in the contemporary world at which he had finally arrived. He gives us to understand, first of all, that something horrendous and utterly unprecedented has come to pass. It happened in 1963, when that Black Mass was celebrated in the Chapel of St. Paul within the walls of the Vatican: since that moment in history, what Malachi Martin terms a "superforce" has been operative, wreaking havoc upon the Church. The first objective of this satanic intrusion, we are told, is to neutralize the Papacy: "The aim of the present superforce,"

Malachi Martin tells us quite explicitly, "is to make sure that the Petrine exercise of the keys ceases."[3] And this effective cessation of Papal Primacy, he goes on to explain, is in fact lethal: "The Church will never be restored as it was. That is dead and gone. We're going to entombment before we get to the resurrection."[4] The central and most vital element, moreover, that has in effect been destroyed is precisely the Mass: the so-called Tridentine, or Roman, as Malachi Martin prefers to call it. And as he goes on to explain: "There *is* no other real Mass in the Roman rite." Here we have it: this is the crucial fact, the key recognition upon which everything turns! Our salvation was wrought on Calvary: "and deep down they [the architects and aficionados of the New Order] are expressing Lucifer's own hatred for Calvary, because the Mass *is* Calvary."[5]

As regards the new or "reformed" liturgy, the so-called Novus Ordo Mass, the crucial point to be made is that Calvary has in effect been excised—or at the very least rendered "optional"—by exceedingly artful means: following in the foot-steps of Martin Luther one has effected a shift from the authentic Sacrifice to a communal celebration of sorts, a kind of "memorial" meal. Now, it appears that Malachi Martin did not go so far as to pronounce the Novus Ordo Mass invalid *per se*; yet he did think that it *tended* to be: "If you ask me my personal opinion, I believe that the majority of Novus Ordo Masses are invalid, for one reason or another."[6] He was further convinced that Annibale Bugnini's liturgical creation was disastrous in its overall effect: "I think the New Mass is the fountainhead of all our difficulties."[7] The Novus Ordo Mass constitutes, after all, the heart and center

---

[3] *Catholicism Overturned*, p. 25. All eight interviews are available in CD or booklet form from Triumph Communications, PO Box 479, Davidson, SK, S0G 1A0, Canada.
[4] Ibid., p. 33.
[5] *The Deserted Vineyard*, p. 27.
[6] *Crossing the Desert*, p. 41.
[7] *Catholicism Overturned*, p. 41.

of what may thus be termed the Novus Ordo Church, what Malachi Martin refers to perspicaciously as "a new church within the Church": a man-made church founded in the wake of Vatican II, which "is actually an anti-Church."

This brings us at last to the so-called "underground Church," a subject we need to comprehend with precision: for this in a way represents the "Church of the entombment" and constitutes moreover the domain in which Malachi Martin exercised his priestly ministry in his later years. The decisive fact, he tells us, is that "the *real* Church is going underground." Unbeknownst to the vast majority of Catholics, clergy and laity alike, an authentically *Catholic* "underground" Church, based upon the Roman rite of Mass, has already sprung into existence:

> If you want to gauge the ignorance of the bishops and the myopia of this Pope [he is referring to John Paul II], then come with me sometime and visit the underground Church in the United States. If only the bishops and the Pope knew the extent of the underground Church! There is an underground network of Masses, baptisms, confessions, bishops, priests, nuns, seminaries, and libraries.... It is a small minority, but it is spreading everywhere....[8]

Here at last we catch a glimpse of what had apparently become the prime object of Malachi Martin's ministry. Not only as a priest did he labor in behalf of the "underground" Church, but also by offering financial assistance to struggling priests, religious communities of disenfranchised nuns, and other casualties of the New Order. As we learned by chance when we met him in 1997, he now supported 49 former diocesan priests who had been unceremoniously cast into the street by their bishops because they refused to discard the Roman rite of Mass.

What is ultimately at stake in that ministry is the preservation of the authentic Sacramental Order of the Catholic Church, above all the Holy Sacrifice of the Mass. And one should add that

[8] *The Deserted Vineyard*, p. 55.

in the decades following Vatican II, not a few highly placed prelates in Rome were in fact keenly aware of this crucial necessity. As Malachi Martin explains, referring to a Cardinal named Alfons Stickler, who "has no power, but does his best":

> We must get back to the original form of the Mass. We have to reform the entire structure of the Church that we have built since Vatican II. That is what he said quite plainly. If you speak to Cardinal Gagnon, who is retired, he says the same thing. If you speak to Cardinal Oddi, he says the same thing. If you speak to Cardinal Ciappi, he says the same thing. But they are all retired and they are all helpless.[9]

The difference, let it be noted, is that Malachi Martin was *not* retired—and could not *be* retired—nor was he helpless in the least: he proceeded rather, with astounding intelligence and indefatigable energy, to protect and foster what was left of the authentic Catholic Church: that, evidently, was his objective. The decisive fact, however, is that such a restoration could no longer be accomplished "from inside." Let us remember: there was now, emplaced in the Vatican, a "superforce" missioned precisely to thwart any such endeavor.

The question presents itself, of course, how something as unthinkable as a satanic "powergrab" capable of shutting down "the Petrine exercise of the keys" could conceivably take place in the Church founded by Christ Himself; and it happens that there is a definitive answer to this formidable question, given by the Blessed Virgin Mary herself, which tells us all we need to know. Let me remind the reader of two well-known facts relating to the Fatima revelations. The first is the double request of Our Lady, directed to the Conciliar Popes, to disclose the so-called Third Secret and consecrate Russia to Her Immaculate Heart—neither of which has been accomplished to this day. Which brings us to the second fact: Our Lady's warning, namely, that if Her request

---

[9] Ibid., p. 53.

is not fulfilled, a "diabolical disorientation" would descend upon the Church. Now, as all who have eyes can see, this is precisely what did come to pass: it was presumably the failure on the part of at least John XXIII to obey the commands of the *Theotokos* Herself that opened the Vatican to the precincts of Hell on June 29, 1963, eight days after the election of Paul VI. And thus began an era of ecclesiastical subversion without precedent in the history of the Church, characterized by a pervasive disorientation that is in truth *diabolical*.

There is, finally, one more observation that needs to be made, which moreover relates specifically to the present book: Malachi Martin's mission, it appears, extends in the final count beyond what he terms "the Church of the entombment" to that of the Resurrection. He gives us namely a foretaste, if you will, of that consummate Catholicity which transcends the didactic modes and scholastic formulations familiar to us from the past. The rest, our Catholic faith assures us, will be accomplished in good time by Christ Himself as He guides the Church—His beloved Bride!—from the darkness of "entombment" to the splendor of her Resurrection.

Index

About the Authors

After graduating from Cornell University at age 18 with majors in physics, mathematics, and philosophy, Wolfgang Smith went on to receive an M.S. in physics from Purdue University and a Ph.D. in mathematics from Columbia. He pursued a career as a professor of mathematics and taught at various universities, including M.I.T. and U.C.L.A. Smith is best known for his pioneering work pertaining to the ontological interpretation of quantum theory and his subsequent critique of the contemporary scientistic world-view.

Malachi Martin began his adult life as a member of the Jesuit order. He obtained a doctorate in archeology, Oriental studies, and Semitic languages from the Catholic University of Louvain. Fr. Martin pursued a brilliant research career in paleography and related fields, taught at the Pontifical Biblical Institute, and served as private secretary to Cardinal Bea. Later he gained renown as the bestselling author of *Hostage to the Devil*, *The Jesuits*, *The Windswept House*, and many other works.